CountryLiving
Cottage Style

Country Living
Cottage Style

MARIE PROELLER HUESTON

HEARST BOOKS
New York

HEARST BOOKS
New York

An Imprint of Sterling Publishing
387 Park Avenue South
New York, NY 10016

This book was previously published as a hardcover under the title *Cottage Style*, 978-1-58816-108-6.

Design by: Matthew Papa

Library of Congress Cataloging-in-Publication Data available upon request

10 9 8 7 6 5 4 3 2

Country Living is a trademark of Hearst Communications, Inc.
www.countryliving.com

For information about custom editions, special sales, premium and corporate purchases, please contact Sterling Special Sales Department at 800-805-5489 or specialsales@sterlingpub.com.

Distributed in Canada by Sterling Publishing
c/o Canadian Manda Group, 165 Dufferin Street
Toronto, Ontario, Canada M6K 3H6

Distributed in Australia by Capricorn Link (Australia) Pty. Ltd.
P.O. Box 704, Windsor, NSW 2756 Australia

Manufactured in China

Sterling ISBN 978-1-58816-873-3

PAGE 1 **A perfect example of mismatched elements coming together to create an inviting whole, this headboard and bedside table work together beautifully. The scalloped edges of the pillowcase complement the gracefully turned legs of the side table. The milk glass lamp dates from the 1930s.**
PAGE 2 **White matelasse bedspreads and Double Wedding Ring quilts dress the 1940s twin beds in the guest room of this Long Island cottage. The interlocking circles of the quilts mirror the pattern on the rose-print wallpaper. Attic space was eliminated to give the cottage's cozy bedrooms an airy feeling.**

contents

introduction

OPPOSITE Although most cottage gardens feature a veritable patchwork of colorful blooms, some homeowners choose one beloved flower and plant it in profusion. Hydrangeas were the blossom of choice for this cottage owner. A patch of grass and breathing space between each hydrangea bush keep the look from overtaking this small plot.

Decorating trends come and go, but America's fascination with cottages has endured for nearly two centuries. The range of interpretations that can be found—from sunny California bungalows decorated with flea-market finds to cedar-shingled Nantucket dwellings filled with nautical antiques to wood-paneled Adirondack cabins boasting wide stone hearths—is certainly a large part of the appeal. Equally important are the human scale and relaxed atmosphere of these homes, benefits for anyone seeking a respite from the hustle and bustle of everyday life. Whatever the reason, one thing is certain: Cottage style is here to stay.

One might imagine that to inspire such devotion a dwelling would need to be grand, imposing, and ornately furnished. Quite the opposite is true. For no matter where it's located or what style its architectural elements possess, the cottage is universally humble, cozy, and above all, imbued with an unassuming charm all its own. Clearly, a cottage is more than four walls and the possessions within them; it is a complete seduction of the senses.

The attraction begins the instant the home's exterior comes into view, triggering long-buried memories of fairy-tale houses nestled in forests and sun-warmed kitchens of beloved grandparents. Crossing the threshold, visitors are drawn nearer, beckoned to roam from room to room, to sink into an overstuffed armchair, to inspect the treasures filling the dining-room hutch, or to rest beside a bright windowsill and watch butterflies flutter through the flower garden. Nowhere else are the seemingly incongruous emotional states of serenity and joyful expectation as artfully conjured.

We can thank the British aristocracy of the eighteenth and nineteenth centuries for sparking the Western world's love affair with the cottage. It was this group of people who first recognized the intrinsic beauty of the simple dwellings inhabited by country craftsmen, merchants, and farmers. Many wealthy landowners commissioned architects to design similar living quarters—often replete with such classic details as thatched roofs, ivy-covered walls, and latticework windows—for their gardeners, gamekeepers, and coachmen. One-room cottages even became common garden elements akin to gazebos and hedge mazes, providing a country gentleman with an idyllic spot to retire to for an hour or so.

As the nineteenth century progressed, the cottage became a symbol of the slower-paced rural way of life that was increasingly threatened by the advancements of industrialization, adding a nostalgic glow to the small structure's growing popularity. Across the Atlantic, Victorian America embraced cottage style with the same fervor with which it greeted anything pertaining to hearth and home. Not only

OPPOSITE LEFT Filling a pitcher with flowers highlights its graceful form and imbues a room with cottage style. Here, an ironstone pitcher spills over with delicate pink roses.

OPPOSITE RIGHT A cozy breakfast nook at the end of a galley kitchen offers a place to eat, read the paper, or do homework. Comfortable wing chairs, a rustic painted table, and a collection of pottery on the windowsill add personal touches.

ABOVE A fresh twist on book display: Volumes are stacked on their sides, creating eye-catching columns in the living room. A collection of Victorian paintings lines the top of the bookcase (roses were a favorite subject for amateur artists in the nineteenth century). When displaying collections, whether still-life paintings or green vases, grouping a few great pieces together heightens the visual impact.

did the Americans appreciate the buildings' aesthetic qualities, they also admired what they perceived to be the moral virtues of these modest houses. "What an unfailing barrier against vice, immorality, and bad habits," opined landscape designer Andrew Jackson Downing in his 1842 book, *Victorian Cottage Residences*, "are those tastes which lead us to embellish a home whose humble roof, whose shady porch, whose verdant lawn and smiling flowers, all breathe forth to us a domestic feeling that at once purifies the heart and binds us more closely to our fellow beings!"

The final element that ensured the cottage's perfect fit with the American way of life was its small scale, a factor that made acquiring a home of one's own an accessible, affordable dream for the nation's burgeoning middle class. Architects gleaned ideas from home and abroad to create efficient, attractive designs: Colonial-style Cape Cods, Carpenter Gothic farmhouses, and English stone cottages, to name a few. One style in particular, the Arts and Crafts bungalow, was so popular during the first two decades of the twentieth century that its columned veranda and broad roof were among the most common sights in suburban areas developed during that period. Ladies' magazines of the day helped spread cottage style throughout the land. Such publications as *Good Housekeeping* and *Ladies' Home Journal* taught homemakers how to outfit interiors in the casual style that best suited cottage living. Furnishings were comfortable and durable, not fussy or difficult to clean. Colors were subdued, upholstery prints and dinnerware patterns pretty. Treasured collections filled cupboards and crannies. And gifts from nature, be they potted plants, dried herbs, or fresh flowers from the garden, provided a finishing touch to the homey scene.

Little has changed in the past hundred years. Twenty-first-century interpretations of cottage style still exude comfort, casualness, and a penchant for pretty objects. There are, however, a few major differences between then and now. For one thing, it's no longer necessary to live in a cottage to enjoy this type of home's myriad charms. Upholstering a city apartment's sofa with an exuberant cabbage-rose print, employing an iron bed frame in the guest room of a suburban split-level ranch, or arranging a collection of framed botanical prints on one wall of a lakeside cabin will instill laid-back cottage spirit in each of these dwellings.

Another difference is that homeowners today sprinkle a healthy amount of humor into this old-fashioned decorating style. Hang a crystal chandelier in a country dining room? Incomprehensible a century ago. Now, whimsical combinations of patterns, colors, textures, and materials abound. It's no wonder, then, that cottages are often furnished with flea-market finds. Many of the items commonly found at flea markets are well-suited to cottage living, including both objects that can still be used for their original purposes (a rose-motif tea set, an alabaster lamp, a needle-point footstool) and ones that can be re-imagined (vintage tea towels hung at a bathroom window or a garden bench pressed into service as a coffee table). Pieces that can be used for storage such as roomy dressers, bookcases, and armoires are especially desirable finds: A fresh coat of paint is usually all that's needed to breathe new life into them.

RIGHT Porches can set the tone for what's beyond the front door, as this porch does for a 1914 California bungalow decorated with flea-market finds. The homeowner's knack for finding secondhand treasures extended to the vintage hotel chairs she found to furnish the porch. Embellished with plush pillows, the inviting space is the perfect place to spend a leisurely afternoon visiting with neighbors.

Country Living Cottage Style salutes both traditional takes and contemporary twists on this enduring look. In the following pages, you'll visit dozens of homes and glimpse countless notions. We'll highlight essential elements that make a room "cottage"; showcase everyday interiors transformed into charming oases by their creative owners; and provide tips on choosing the best cottage-style furnishings, reviving secondhand finds, and displaying cherished objects throughout the house.

living rooms

"Have nothing in your houses that you do not know to be useful, or believe to be beautiful." Never do Arts and Crafts reformer William Morris's words seem more significant than when considering the cottage and, more specifically, the cottage living room. Usefulness is of the essence here. Although space is limited, guests should be as graciously accommodated as possible. Beauty cannot be overlooked either, for as the most public room in the house, the living room should be a repository for your favorite things—objects that reveal your personality, your pastimes, and your passions.

When the owners' dream mantel turned out to be too narrow for the hearth, they commissioned a carpenter to widen it. The cupboards flanking the fireplace were built from salvaged wood, giving them an authentic old-fashioned look. Frequently seen at flea markets, small tables and trunks like those seen here can be used in myriad ways around the house.

Before a single piece of furniture can be brought in, the room itself must be analyzed. Look first at your walls. What color would best suit the space and best complement your collections? For many cottage owners, some variation of white (pearl, eggshell, cream) is the color of choice. Not only do white walls make small spaces appear larger, they also offer no competition for the furnishings or objects placed against them. (No wonder they're so common in art galleries.) For others, though, all white seems a bit cold. These people might choose a barely there shade of blue, yellow, gray, or sage green. Pale hues still make a room feel bigger and might even accentuate deeper tones of sky blue, ocher, charcoal, or hunter green found in the furniture.

By and large, paint is used more often than wallpaper in cottage living rooms because of space constraints. When papering is chosen, however, prints tend to be tiny or softly colored. Hanging wallpaper above wainscoting or beaded-board paneling is one way to keep a lively print from overpowering a room. Turn your attention next to floors and windows. Cottages with wonderful old pine, oak, or maple floorboards are highly admired. Most homeowners keep wood floors uncovered and lightly polished, taking care to protect high-traffic areas with runners in hallways and area rugs in front of sofas and beneath dining tables. Other people prefer to cover floors, perhaps opting for wall-to-wall sisal or a plush carpet in a cheerful color. Woven and hooked rugs, whether genuine antiques or new pieces made in the traditional manner, work especially well in cottage living rooms because they can reflect colors and textures found elsewhere in the room.

Bay windows are natural spots to focus attention in the cottage home. In this living room, smaller-scale furnishings were chosen to fit the sunny space between the windows. A blue-and-white color scheme unifies the different fabric patterns used on the comfortable love seat and the upholstered bench doubling as a coffee table. Dark wood blinds at the windows echo the mahogany side table and furniture feet. Wall-to-wall sisal is an easy way to give a room a finished look.

Windows, too, can be handled in a number of different ways. Shades or shutters offer a streamlined look to complement pared-down interiors. One popular option is white shades or shutters set against white window trim; another choice is a tone of wood (walnut, ash, maple) that matches other wooden furnishings in the room. If flowing drapes or pretty patterned curtains are more your style, consider one of the following design options. Curtain fabric can identically match a fabric pattern in the room (a rose print both at the windows and on the sofa) or it might share a similar color scheme while displaying a different motif (blue-and-white toile curtains beside a chair upholstered in a blue-and-white check, for instance). Some owners even choose to leave windows bare in a cottage living room. While this approach lets in abundant sunlight and draws attention to the architectural detailing, it works best in homes in rural areas or on ample property where privacy is not an issue.

While there are certain furnishings that typify the cottage look, no particular style need be excluded from this type of decorating. A classic interior usually includes an overstuffed, slipcovered sofa and one or two matching armchairs. These items work well because they are extremely comfortable, easy to care for, and seem to extend an immediate invitation to all who pass by to sit down and relax. Rustic furnishings that capture the spirit of the great outdoors also work well in the cottage living room. Homeowners who love the rustic look have been known to flank a fireplace with Adirondack porch chairs or to position a wicker rocking chair beside a plant-stand-turned-side-table. If more formal designs appeal to you, don't despair:

Blue and white is one of the most popular color combinations of all time—and it's easy to see why. Fresh stripes cover the sofa and armchairs in this sunny living room. Pillows made from vintage ticking stripe and a checkered tablecloth add a touch of old to the new. A painted garden bench runs the length of the double window, keeping beloved books and collections within easy reach. Above the window, a peg rail becomes a whimsical and unexpected curtain rod. Minimally adorned white walls and a whitewashed floor covered with a woven rug provide contrast to the dark wood ceiling.

Graceful wood-framed settees and slipper chairs upholstered in chintz can work just as well.

Many people even enjoy combining casual and formal elements into a cohesive whole. A welcoming seating area might be created from such disparate furnishings as an antique chaise longue dressed in a pretty red-rose print and a pair of red metal patio chairs from the 1950s. The complementary color scheme unites the two styles. Or imagine an all-white living room with an elegantly tufted sofa and an apple-green garden bench employed as a coffee table for a pop of color in the center of the scene. Cottage style encourages such unconventional arrangements, as long as there are thought and purpose behind the choices.

With all the roles that living rooms are expected to perform these days, it's also worthwhile mentioning that storage pieces of all shapes will prove themselves enormously helpful. In place of a traditional coffee table, for example, a blanket chest or ottoman with storage space can hold board games, photo albums, or warm throws. A corner cabinet or glass-front cupboard can double as a bookcase or as a repository for curios. A sturdy basket beside the fireplace can store children's toys, while a stack of vintage tins can organize stationery. Possibilities abound.

Once the furniture is in place, collections are the next detail to ponder. Beloved objects can either be incorporated into more practical arrangements (like bud vases beside a row of garden books) or given a space all their own, such as an entire cupboard filled with ironstone or a curio cabinet filled with figurines. A mantel is a particularly good place to showcase possessions because it is a spot to which the

The color scheme and furnishings in this nineteenth-century Maine cottage have been kept simple, creating a comfortable yet gracious setting. The graceful silhouettes of the coffee table, sofa, and two chairs make an elegant composition. The vintage wallpaper provides a patterned backdrop for the neutral color palette, while the gauzy curtains filter sunlight. Natural textiles add visual warmth to the space.

eye is naturally drawn. A wonderful collection of books, too, should be given a place of honor in the cottage living room. Built-in bookcases are a desirable feature, but if your home lacks this detail, alternatives include a standing bookcase, a hanging shelf, or a short glass-front cabinet. Piles of art books can also be placed around the room on tabletops (ideally beside a comfortable chair) so guests can flip through them at their leisure. If your book collection is large enough, you could even create a small table beside a sofa or chair by piling broad volumes one on top of the other.

The finishing touch to the cottage living room is artwork on the walls. In the traditional English cottage, framed prints of botanical studies, historical events, animals—especially dogs—and domestic scenes often covered walls in a haphazard manner. Today, displays tend to be sparser—highlighting a single row of botanical prints, for instance, or a small cluster of silhouettes. The area above a mantel is a natural place for a large painting, print, or photograph. Landscapes, marine paintings, floral studies, and animal portraits are all popular choices for this spot. The wall space over a sofa can be daunting to fill: Try a row of three or four similarly framed prints (botanicals or Currier and Ives–style images, for example) or an arrangement of family photographs in frames big and small. Sometimes hammer-shy homeowners choose not to hang anything at all. In such cases, artwork can be lined up on a mantel or side table, creating visual interest without pounding a single nail into a wall. The choice is entirely up to you.

OPPOSITE Even though the living room in their lakeside retreat was decidedly cozy, the owners wanted plenty of comfortable seating for guests. Their solution was to position two overstuffed sofas on either side of the room; crisp white slipcovers keep the large furnishings from overpowering the small space. An ottoman performs triple duty as footrest, coffee table, and additional seating. Built-in bookcases flank the river-stone hearth, providing much-needed storage. The tops of the bookcases align with the mantel, creating one long shelf on which to display a collection of black-and-white photographs.

mixing and matching fabrics

Layering different fabric patterns can energize a room, but avoiding a look that's too busy can be tricky. To begin, choose a complementary color scheme (red and white or blue and white, for example) to unify varying prints like toiles, plaids, and stripes. Limit yourself to one or two dominant hues in a single setting—such as the red and purple seen here—to prevent overpowering arrangements.

RIGHT Generous coats of cream paint were applied to pine paneling to make this living room appear more spacious. The shade of green chosen for the bookshelves, mantel, and trim matches a favorite collection of plates now displayed on the wall and also complements the yellow and apple-green furnishings. Framed botanical prints, potted plants, and floral-motif pillows attest to the owner's passion for gardening. Family photographs and heirlooms like the 1930s mirror above the fireplace are scattered around the room. When the owners first moved in, wall-to-wall carpeting covered the home's original chestnut flooring. A good sanding and an application of polyurethane brought the floors back to life.

RIGHT Every cottage needs an over-stuffed armchair for its owner (or a guest) to flop into and relax. Plush pillows and a soft, warm throw are essential to attain the utmost comfort and to ward off any unwelcome drafts. Hatboxes covered in ticking stripe provide clever and attractive storage.

window seats

Whether your goal is time alone with a cup of tea and a new novel or quality time with young children and a picture book, few spots in the home are as inviting as a window seat. From this cushioned perch, you can look into the room and absorb all the comforts of home. You can also gaze into the garden or out onto a bustling street and let your mind wander as far as it wishes to go. If your home does not already have a window seat, adding one will ensure hours of enjoyment for you and your family.

Bay windows are perhaps the most natural spots to transform. Owing to the bay window's shape, a seat can be constructed without using any extra space in the room—a plus in small dwellings. Standard windows can also become window seats, but placement here will require a little planning if the seats are to appear as they most often do—as if set into the wall. A simple way to achieve this much-loved style in front of a standard window is to build wide bookshelves on either side, leaving space for a seat in between. Although this design eats up a bit more room space, the additional bookshelves make up for it: You can never have too many bookshelves in a cottage interior.

Carpenters (or handy homeowners) can easily take window and room measurements and purchase wood for the project at a local lumberyard. Be sure to design your window seat with storage space in mind. Under-seat storage (accessible either by a lift top or cabinet doors facing the room) is an ideal spot for toys, board games, and sports equipment. For a seamless appearance, paint the window seat's frame to match the trim color in the room. A window seat in a room with white trim, for example, looks best when painted white; a seat in a room with green trim will look lovely in a matching shade of green. As a finishing touch, order custom-slipcovered cushions from an upholstery shop or a website you like. Fabric patterns that match existing drapery or sofa covers are a good option. Another choice would be a solid hue that complements other furnishings in the room.

RIGHT If space permits, invite guests to peruse your book collection by placing favorite titles on an accessible table. Here, armchairs covered in the same soft lavender fabric as the drapes await occupants, while a leather ottoman stashed neatly beneath the table can be brought out in a flash whenever a footrest or additional seating is needed. A potted orchid, fresh roses in a crystal vase, and a bowl of potpourri introduce elements of nature to the indoor setting.

OPPOSITE Collections have been pared down and colors turned up a notch to create this elegant twist on the cottage interior. Striped upholstery continues the room's clean lines without forfeiting comfort. On the mantel, a large framed photograph and three smaller landscapes make a pleasing, condensed arrangement. A tiered metal stand in the corner elevates everyday items—tin buckets, a gazing ball, and a wire basket—to works of art by allowing viewers to see their sculptural qualities.

slipcovered furniture

The benefits of slipcovers in the home are many. Foremost among them is that these easy-to-care-for covers allow you to have elegant pieces of furniture positioned prominently in the living room, swathed in the colors and patterns you love, without having to worry about random spills or children's sticky fingers. Just zip off the outermost layer of fabric and into the wash it goes—that's what makes slipcovers such an essential part of casual, comfortable cottage style. Another plus is the fact that slipcovers fashioned from the same pattern, color, or family of colors can unify different styles of sofas, armchairs, slipper chairs, and ottomans, creating a harmonious look without having to spend extra money for a matching suite of furniture. Changing only the slipcovers is also a budget-conscious way to give a room a whole new look. Likewise, keeping an extra set of slipcovers on hand allows you to dramatically alter the mood of a room depending on the season. White covers add seashore style to a home in the summertime; hunter-green or deep-red covers look wonderfully warm and cozy around the holidays. Slipcovers made from a large, single sheet of fabric (available through a number of mail-order catalogues these days) work well if you want to try a new look just for a season, as these options are simple to drape on any sofa and are less expensive and easier to store than a full set of slipcovers.

Most decorating sources offer custom slipcovers from their upholstery departments. If you are in the market for new furniture, bring swatches of the drapery pattern or paint color with you so you can choose a complementary fabric. Keep in mind that certain fabrics are easier to care for than others. Cotton twills and denims are the most worry-free, since these can be put in the washing machine. Damasks and velvets will likely require dry cleaning. If looking to order new slipcovers for furniture you already own, the same stores can usually send an upholstery expert to your home to take measurements and make slipcovers in a matter of weeks. Another option (for sewing aficionados) is to make your own slipcovers. Craft books available in bookstores can lead you through the entire process, from choosing the best fabrics to using the proper weight needles and thread.

ABOVE Decorated with eighteenth- and nineteenth-century antiques, this cozy sitting room has a simple, serene ambience, thanks to its soft and muted color scheme. The pleasing palette of blue and neutral shades unifies the striped, toile, and floral designs used in the room, while the neutral carpet grounds the mix of patterns.

BELOW This 1920s house underwent a total renovation—which included breaking down several interior walls— and now features newly opened-up rooms unified by a simple palette that visually links them throughout the home. The sofa is covered in mid-1800s homespun, and the comfy chair is slipcovered. A Scandinavian-style grandfather clock is a striking element in the room. The various shades of white and stone hues create a sense of serenity throughout the space.

RIGHT To create the pleasing mantel-top arrangement, clusters of collections were placed on both sides of a family portrait (mercury glass on one side, green McCoy pottery on the other). The mantel was custom-built for the space and is a reproduction of an antique design spotted at a Paris flea market. The armchair rocker was a $25 tag-sale find; new beige-and-white striped slipcovers gave it a new lease on life.

a picture-perfect cottage

OPPOSITE The key to blending different fabric patterns successfully is to stick with a cohesive color scheme, like the living room's pleasing combination of white, red, and green. Faded blue paint on the coffee table and wooden bucket adds a little extra color to the room.

When photographers take a picture, they check to see that all elements are arranged correctly within the frame before pressing down on the shutter. When two photographers renovate a cottage, you can be sure the result will be equally well composed. Such is the case with this Burbank, California, bungalow. The 1923 structure was in poor shape when the owners first laid eyes on it, but it had "good bones" and ample property surrounding it to transform the cozy quarters into a more spacious interior that could comfortably accommodate the couple and their two young sons. The kitchen and master bedroom were expanded, a new staircase was constructed, and a third bedroom was added upstairs, increasing the overall space from 1,250 to 2,400 square feet.

After the dust had settled from the renovation, the owners set about creating rooms that would reflect their unique sense of style while remaining firmly rooted in the past. In much of the living space, warm ecru paint was chosen for the walls. Beaded-board paneling covering the lower part of the walls was whitewashed and then gently distressed to mirror the surfaces on the antique and vintage furniture the owners love so dearly. One room where strong color and pattern stand out is the kitchen, where a graphic black-and-white wallpaper pattern makes a bold statement. Wood floors were painted, pale gray in some rooms and, in others, in a large checkerboard pattern of pale green and worn white. The effect of soft hues on floors as well as walls visually enlarges small spaces.

OPPOSITE To keep the kitchen's bold rooster wallpaper from overwhelming the room, white beaded-board paneling was used on the lower portion of the walls, and cabinets and floors were painted white and pale gray, respectively. The black on the walls is reflected in the countertops, table, and iron chairs.

When it came time to choose fabrics for window treatments and upholstery, the owners turned to their sizable collection of vintage swatches. Cream-colored damask, striped patterns in varying widths, and crisp white linen were chosen for the curtains, which function more as decorative details than privacy providers. The variety of materials and patterns at the windows adds visual interest in each room. The owners' fabric collection also provided a lively mix of florals, stripes, and checks to upholster the living room sofa as well as chairs and pillows throughout the house. Different as they may be, the fabrics share a unifying color scheme: off-white, wheat, and faded red.

Common threads can also be spotted in the cottage's furniture, arranged with care by those exacting photographers' eyes. Worn finishes and faded fabrics are seen in abundance, as are pieces that have been repurposed: a deck chair from an ocean liner has become an armchair in the living room, while a blanket chest doubles as a coffee table. Black wrought-iron furniture and accessories appear not only in the kitchen, but in the living room and bath as well—a good way to reference the bold black background of the kitchen wallpaper elsewhere in the house. As a final note, whimsical touches such as crystal chandeliers and everyday objects displayed in an artistic manner (antique shears hung on the wall, a weathered oar suspended from the ceiling) ensure that formal and informal elements blend into a cohesive whole.

LEFT A storage room built around an outdoor barbecue pit became the dining room. Standing in the center of the space is an oak table that was left behind by the home's previous owners. To revive the curvaceous piece, the base was painted and distressed, and the top marbleized.

ABOVE In a guest bedroom, worn surfaces unify the vintage headboard and nightstand; the sage green of the walls complements both pieces. Vintage linens on overstuffed pillows, along with a pretty patchwork quilt, create an inviting look for the bed.

CHAPTER 2

kitchens &
dining areas

The cottage kitchen is often the heart of the home, and its decor can reflect any style you can imagine. Do typical English cottages appeal to you? If so, your kitchen might feature lace at the windows, a deep soapstone sink, tile floors, and an ornate gas lamp (converted to electric) suspended above a round oak table and chairs. If a 1940s Cape Cod is more to your liking, try gingham curtains, a porcelain double sink, linoleum flooring (yes, it is still made), and a chrome-and-milk-glass lamp over an enamel-topped table and chrome-and-vinyl side chairs. Even a modern aesthetic can find its

Although the owner of this Bucks County, Pennsylvania, home updated the kitchen's appliances and installed new butcher-block counters, he left the original hand-carved scrollwork surrounding the window intact. The quaint detail adds oodles of charm to the modest space and acts as a decorative frame for the view through the window.

ABOVE In kitchens that lack sufficient cabinet space, large cupboards are essential for storage. Both antique designs and newly made pieces can be found in a range of sizes and colors to suit your home. Storing flatware in small pots and tumblers is a terrific way to show off decorative handles.

OPPOSITE Ideas for using old items in new ways abound in this welcoming kitchen: Tea towels have been transformed into curtains that coordinate with the soft-green walls, a garden urn holds utensils in the center of the room, baskets in a cubby beside the sink can hold table linens or dry goods, a vintage chalkboard becomes a reusable surface for shopping lists and phone messages, and coat hooks hold colanders and tea towels on the wall. Plus, a hamper-turned-garbage-can proves that trash receptacles don't always need to be hidden away under the sink. Open shelves display a collection of ironstone pitchers and a lovely set of brown-and-white transferware. To increase work space without limiting floor space, the owners chose a narrow work island; mixing bowls and serving pieces are stored on the open shelf below.

way into the cottage kitchen in the form of industrial pendant lamps, stainless-steel appliances, and a pared-down, uncluttered look.

Before the cottage became an established architectural style, kitchens in homes of taste were situated away from the public areas of the residence—in many cases, stowed away in the basement or in a separate structure altogether. At the time, cooking odors that permeated the house were a homemaker's worst nightmare. Over the years, the stature of the kitchen has grown. The compact size of the cottage home may have had something to do with it. Without ample space for an off-site or basement-level room, cottage kitchens were integrated into the first-floor layout. Placed at the back of the house and afforded plenty of windows for cross ventilation, the kitchen soon became a favorite family gathering place. Nowadays, even dinner guests love to linger here while the host and hostess prepare the food. (Small wonder, then, that upholstered armchairs have become a common sight in kitchens. A wing chair in the kitchen would have confounded the nineteenth-century homemaker!)

To assess the cottage potential in any kitchen, you must first analyze the available storage space. Because square footage can often be limited, be sure there are plenty of cabinets and shelves for everyday dinnerware and kitchen collectibles like tin canisters, enamelware coffeepots, and Jaydite mixing bowls. For older homes that lack period cabinetry, new designs with an old-fashioned look can be purchased or commissioned from a cabinetmaker. If all-new cabinets strain your decorating budget, give common wood cabinets an antique look by painting (white or any color) and gently distressing with sandpaper. Many devotees of the cottage

OPPOSITE The shade of green chosen for cupboards and cabinets in this kitchen may be old-fashioned in feeling, but the sleek brushed-chrome appliances and retro lighting inject a decidedly modern sensibility into the space. Glass-front cabinets and open shelving provide plenty of room to display a large pottery collection. A white tile backsplash and marble countertops are clean and serious in tone; the zig-zag trim above the window and along the base of the work island is just for fun. In addition to their aesthetic qualities, marble counters are also a great choice for people who love to bake. The lavender bar stools add an extra dash of color to the room.

style opt for glass-front cabinet doors to showcase china and glassware. Others dismiss cabinets altogether and instead build open shelves throughout the room to display collections and everyday wares for all to see.

Once you've assessed the storage situation, turn your attention to the colors that will coat walls and woodwork. Light hues open up tight spaces, which explains why white and pale pastels are so common in the cottage kitchen. You might decide to keep the walls white and paint the cabinetry and woodwork blue or green. Wallpaper is not unheard of in the cottage kitchen, though it is usually used sparingly—on the upper portion of the wall above white beaded-board paneling, for example. Cheerful floral motifs or narrow stripes in soothing tones are two possibilities to consider.

Windows and floors are frequently kept simple in cottage kitchens, some-times being left entirely bare. Unfettered windows allow sunlight to flood the room, while floors free of rugs are as easy-care as they come. When they are adorned, windows often wear half curtains of white eyelet, lace, or a pretty pattern that co-ordinates with the colors found in the room. Area rugs on the floor are most often found in front of the sink or stove and take the form of colorful hooked rugs or other woven designs. Checkerboard floor patterns, whether fashioned from lino-leum or painted or stained onto wood, offer an old-fashioned look that has never gone out of style.

Salvage shops are good hunting grounds when renovating or updating a cottage kitchen. Deep sinks are particularly desirable finds, as are sturdy old cabi-nets and vintage lighting fixtures. Even the smallest details found in these shops—glass and porcelain cabinet knobs, decorative tiles, and old hooks that can be used

A singular palette of pale green provides continuity between the living and dining rooms of this small Cape Cod cottage. The tie-on slipcovers were devised to show off the dark wood of the chairs and for ease of removal for washing. The bay window—embellished with a pleated-flange cushion—allows loads of sunlight into the serene room.

to hang dish towels—can add personality to a room. Be sure to carry dimensions with you, especially if you are searching for large items like sinks, and take into account any additional work time that will be needed to revive cabinets or other items coated with layers of paint.

Another reason that the kitchen's importance has increased in the cottage home is the fact that when floor plans do include a separate and distinct room for formal dining, the space is frequently usurped for use as a home office or an extra bedroom. Thus, the kitchen steps in as a room for meals. In homes where the dining room can be used for its original purpose, consider making it as grand as possible, though never ostentatious. Position a tall hutch with a timeworn painted surface or a warm wood stain against the wall, and fill it with your favorite set of china, the rose-pattern teacups you inherited from your grandmother, or knick-knacks collected over the years. The table and chairs can be casual and grand at the same time: Consider a farm table (as long as will comfortably fit) flanked by two long benches and topped with a tower of shiny apples in a repurposed garden urn, or a whitewashed round table, toile seat covers on whitewashed chairs, toile drapes at the windows, and a beautiful flower arrangement in a cranberry-glass vase. In rooms where furnishings are colorful and patterns busy, keep floors clean and simple by choosing sisal carpeting or a woven rug in neutral tones. Boldly patterned rugs stand out in rooms with toned-down furnishings.

RIGHT In the small kitchen of this Cape Cod cottage, slipcovers dress up the stools and add a touch of softness to the hard surfaces around them. The dark wood of the center island provides rich contrast to the white drawers and cupboards underneath and elsewhere in the kitchen. The open shelves in the corner are a perfect spot to display a collection of shapely white pitchers and bowls. A vintage light fixture and mirror over the stove add character to the space.

OPPOSITE A collection of Jade-ite inspired the color choice for this kitchen's walls and work island. To break up the large expanse of white cabinetry, drawer fronts and cabinet-door trim were painted green. Thick butcher block was chosen to top the island, while white tiles cover counters throughout the room. A retro-style double lamp with delicate edges adds a hint of whimsy to this clean-lined setting. A vintage picnic basket kept beside the island is always ready for impromptu outings.

Lighting options vary for both kitchens and dining rooms. Many people position chandeliers directly over the table, and in the modern incarnation of cottages, crystal is just as appropriate as milk glass. Designs with ornate vine or floral motifs also work well in these settings. Recessed lighting is a good option in rooms where ceilings do not afford as much room as you'd like for hanging fixtures or in rooms where a clean-lined look is the goal. Some homeowners combine the two looks, with recessed lighting providing the majority of the room's illumination and a chandelier or vintage-style pendant lamp shedding light on the dining table or work island.

RIGHT Sunflower-yellow paint and a collection of blue-and-white china displayed on the wall bring a bit of Provençal style to this all-American cottage. Bursts of blue are seen elsewhere in the room: in the hanging cupboard to the left of the sink, the wing chair beside the sunny window (an ideal spot to browse through a cookbook), and the ticking-stripe skirt beneath the sink. Sink skirts are an easy way to create additional storage space in small kitchens for trash cans, cleaning supplies, and paper products. Hanging shutters on the window is a nice way to achieve some privacy but still let in plenty of light.

Open shelves are great places to display china and stemware in the kitchen. But don't feel you need to restrict each shelf to a single material—such as all glass on one shelf, for example, and all ceramics on another. This lively grouping combines ironstone, transferware, crystal, copper molds, and an antique wooden potato masher.

Let your kitchen reflect your interests. A passion for gardening and collecting led this owner to choose a fern-print wallpaper and an elegant whitewashed display shelf, complete with towel bar, that can showcase favorite pieces, from an assortment of baskets to treasured linens.

make a message board

Attach a children's chalkboard to an ornate frame discovered at a flea market or garage sale to make a pretty message board for the kitchen, mudroom, or home office. Frames can be painted any color to match the decor of a room. If you can't find the exact size chalkboard for a particular frame, have a piece of plywood cut to size and coat it with chalkboard paint, available at hardware and art-supply stores.

OPPOSITE Whimsical details such as the chandelier combine with traditional pinks and greens to bring a touch of romance to this dining room. The table's "tea cozy" cover and the seat cushions were created from a vintage-style quilt and coordinating floral fabric. A little paint can work magic: The hot pink chairs, fifteen years old, have been painted at least twenty times, and the armoire is repainted whenever the room takes on a new identity.

RIGHT This simple dining area showcases an elegant, Scandinavian-style variation on white-on-white decorating. A thin strip of molding divides the walls into ecru above and beige below. Shield-back side chairs with ticking-stripe seats surround a table whose painted finish reveals the slightest hint of pear green. Walls and floor are kept bare, allowing the graceful lines of the corner cupboard and the abundant ironstone collection found on its shelves to provide all the visual interest the room needs. Centerpieces of seasonal flowers and foliage look stunning when arranged in a large clear-glass vase. Hydrangeas make for a perfect summer bouquet; try daffodils in spring, bittersweet in autumn, and holly in winter.

breakfast nooks

Humble in purpose and size, breakfast nooks are one of the easiest parts of the house to make exquisitely pretty. True breakfast nooks are just that—nooks or alcoves turned into dining spots in space-deprived kitchens. Some feature built-in banquettes with a table in the center, while others accommodate a small table and freestanding chairs. Today we use the term "breakfast nook" more loosely to describe any dining area in a cozy kitchen, whether tucked behind a counter or beside a window. Any small table—square, round, or rectangular—will work here, although whitewashed wood and vintage enamel-topped styles seem especially well suited for the job. Banquettes, short benches, or four-chair sets are all good seating options. Other choices include garden chairs, bistro chairs, or mismatched designs unified by a coat of the same color paint. Window treatments can be old-fashioned in feeling (eyelet or gingham curtains) or more modern (whitewashed wooden blinds or no coverings at all). On the table, printed tablecloths from the 1950s with colorful fruit or flower motifs, or checkered designs in red and white, blue and white, or yellow and white look great. Keep fine china in the dining room, and instead bring out your sturdiest ironstone or everyday china bearing floral patterns or simple stripes of cobalt around the edges. For a finishing touch, arrange garden flowers in a pale-blue canning jar or coffee tin.

Anyone wanting to create an alcove for a breakfast nook in a kitchen that has none can enlist the help of a carpenter, cabinetmaker, or handy friend. Start in a sunny corner of the room—ample light is essential for a nook in which you'll want to linger all morning with a newspaper and coffee. If space is tight, consider building a wall that is flat on the side facing the corner you want to enclose. Line the other side of the wall (the side facing out toward the kitchen) with floor-to-ceiling shelves to create extra storage space for dishes, cookbooks, tin canisters, and accessories. If space permits, you might even consider building a small pantry in place of a wall of shelves. Budget-conscious people can avoid construction costs by positioning a large hutch where the wall would be, facing its back toward the dining area and its shelves toward the kitchen.

The inviting blue-and-white palette and the light and fresh-looking furnishings in this dining room reflect the home's lakeside setting. A bold focal point of the room, the candle chandelier hanging above the pedestal table was found at an antiques store. Aluminum trays, which are affordable Depression-era collectibles, become luminous wall art here. The planked coffered ceiling is a distinctive architectural detail.

ABOVE Pale yellow walls and bright white trim create a cheerful atmosphere in this breakfast area. Open shelves above the windows play host to a collection of floral-motif plates and platters. Three favorite plates are hung with gallery clips to bring visual interest to the far corner of the room. A cabinet unit built out into the room delineates cooking and dining areas and provides additional display space for milk-glass compotes. The small stool comes in handy when dishes need to be retrieved from their roosts or if a third person will be sitting at the table. Because the rest of the room is clean-lined (no curtains, bare floors), the slightly worn surfaces of the whitewashed table and mismatched plank-seat side chairs go virtually unnoticed.

RIGHT When decorating this colorful space, the homeowner sought to re-create the kitchen of her youth. A toned-down shade of turquoise (a classic 1950s color) brightens the breakfast area and echoes the kitchen's cheerful striped wallpaper. Decorative paint techniques were added to the walls (where light sponging produces a cloudlike texture) and the floor (where a trompe l'oeil cat stretches playfully on a checkerboard pattern). Vintage-fabric curtains pick up the yellow from the floor design. Despite their varying shades of yellow, blue, and green, similarly styled side chairs work as a set. A comfortable armchair is upholstered in vintage printed tablecloths and ticking stripe. The table beside the window was made by stacking a blue bed tray on top of a blue garden bench.

ABOVE An old-fashioned bread box adds a touch of cottage to any kitchen. Here, both the green enameled bread box (a flea-market find) and the vase are color coordinated with the collection of Jade-ite dishes, teacups, and saucers. A sense of unity is created by keeping the background color white and accessorizing with one or two predominant colors.

dutch doors

Dutch doors have been a common sight on American farmsteads for centuries. Although the origin of the term is foggy (some trace it back to the Netherlands, others to the Pennsylvania Dutch community), the meaning is the same: Dutch doors are divided horizontally so that the upper and lower parts can operate independently of each other. In the farmhouse, these doors were often found in the front or back doorway. Opening the top of the door would air out the house while maintaining a certain level of privacy and keeping out unwanted critters. With the top open, versions with a small ledge atop the bottom door provided comfortable spots to lean on while talking with neighbors and passersby.

Dutch doors were also used in stables; opening the top would ventilate the stall without setting the livestock free. In today's cottage home, these doors are used most often as back or side doors that open onto a garden or porch. They are especially useful in a kitchen, as leaving the top of the door open will draw out heat and cooking odors while keeping pets inside (or outside, as the case may be). Dutch doors can also be situated in interior doorways. Opening only the top of the door can be helpful in kitchens, home offices, and studios at times when you want to hear what's going on in the rest of the house but would prefer pets and small children stay out.

A fortunate few may discover original Dutch doors in cottage homes. In these cases, a fresh coat of paint may be needed to restore the door to its previous glory. Antique examples sometimes surface at shops specializing in architectural salvage. Bring the doorway dimensions with you when you begin your search, as old doors are sometimes wider than modern doorways. Although the majority of home-improvement stores do not include Dutch doors in their regular stock, most can special order them for you. Prices will likely be higher than standard doors, so calculate the cost into your decorating budget.

Carpenters and cabinetmakers may be able to construct a new Dutch door or to turn an existing door into a Dutch door complete with new hinges and hardware. If a craftsperson does not have his own blueprint, check how-to books in your local bookstore or conduct a Web search for door designs on home-improvement sites.

a victorian seaside cottage

OPPOSITE A double-pedestal table stands at the center of the dining room; the table was custom-designed to match the set of 1950s urn-back chairs that surrounds it. Butter-yellow wing chairs and pale-blue walls call to mind the sand and surf of the cottage's seaside setting.

Victorians were passionate about all things pertaining to home and family, two examples being cottage architecture and vacations by the sea. When these interests coincided, the results were charming residences like the circa 1875 dwelling shown on these pages. Located on Long Island, New York, the front-gabled cottage offered everything its current owners were looking for: a beautiful weekend getaway within driving distance of New York City. The fact that the house needed an extensive renovation did not deter them in the least. Over the course of two years, the owners painted and patched, refinished floors, and scoured salvage shops for sinks, cabinets, lighting, drawer pulls, and doorknobs that fit the style of the house. It was truly a labor of love.

The interior decoration was approached with the same attention to detail as the renovation. The two floors of the house were handled in different ways. The first floor is awash in serene paint colors inspired by nature, including a soft sky blue in the dining room and sage green in the living room. The creamy white kitchen is punctuated by green cabinetry. Pattern is used sparingly on the first floor, making occasional appearances on throw pillows and upholstery or in collections such as the kitchen's brown-and-white transferware china. Windows and floors are left bare (with the exception of sisal carpeting in the living room) to underscore the simple beauty of the house and to allow furniture and collections to take center stage.

In contrast to the solid blocks of color used on the first floor, the upstairs bedrooms are abloom with bold wallpaper patterns. The romantic floral prints are well suited to both the style of the house and the antique and vintage furnishings

that occupy the rooms. In the master bedroom, cheerful purple and yellow hues achieve the owners' goal of a "blooming summertime look" for the room. White bed linens and whitewashed furniture, from the bed frame and dresser to the table and settee, combine to anchor the busy pattern on the walls. Wide-plank wood floors on the second story are left bare, as they were downstairs, and windows are only minimally dressed with white louvered shutters to provide privacy.

Collections of pottery, paintings, and pretty accessories add personality to all rooms. In keeping with the uncluttered look of the house, precious objects are thoughtfully arranged in limited numbers or are kept in enclosed spaces. In some cases they fill glass-front cupboards, such as the assortment of milk glass, white ceramics, and stemware in the dining room and the transferware in the kitchen. In other places, small groupings accent a wall, like the trio of nautical paintings hung in a column in the living room. Placed with purpose, a few items are all it takes to create pretty vignettes in any room.

ABOVE Two smaller bedrooms were combined to make a more spacious master bedroom. The lilac-trellised wallpaper inspired the choice of lavender for the vaulted ceiling and the tufted headboard as well as the selection of buttery yellow upholstery for the settee and side chair.

RIGHT A new bay window brightens the kitchen. Favorite transferware plates are displayed above the window. The brown-and-white palette inspired the fabric choice for the banquette's cushions and throw pillows. Green-glass knobs on the cabinet doors echo the drawers below.

CHAPTER 3

bedrooms

PREVIOUS PAGE This sunny bedroom shows just how easy it is to imbue a city apartment with cottage spirit. Start with a romantic bed—in this case one with a carved-wood-and-cloth headboard—and dress it with linens and quilts and plenty of pillows. Next, hang something delicate at the windows, such as the chambray half curtains seen here. (For extra privacy, a shade could be installed without affecting the window's neat look.) Choose a few favorite items for the wall and arrange them in a casually askew manner, such as the black-and-white photographs of Paris and floral platter between the windows. Finally, add a luxurious detail (maybe a small writing desk like the one at the foot of the bed), and bring a bit of the natural world indoors by lining potted plants along the windowsill.

A lthough every inch of your house should reflect your interests and your own sense of style, the decoration of most rooms will occasionally take other people's needs into account. Is there ample seating for guests around the dinner table? Is there enough space on the coffee table for visitors to rest their drinks? Your bedroom, however, is the one place that is entirely about you. This is the room in which you dream, in which you greet each new day. Passions for roses or lace or even frilly hats that may be toned down elsewhere can be set free here.

An ornate bed frame is the focal point of this light-filled bedroom. Wooden garden furniture like the armchair seen here makes an easy transition indoors when painted white and given a comfortable, boldly striped cushion. A collection of miniature seascapes surrounded by frames made of salvaged wood flanks the closet door.

RIGHT Even the simplest item can make a big impact in a cottage bedroom when you learn to spot the decorative potential in everyday objects. Take a wooden chair like this one, for instance. If you'd spotted it at a flea market with a weathered surface and no seat, you might have walked right past it. Add a pretty, new upholstered cushion and it becomes an attractive addition beside a window or in front of a writing desk.

OPPOSITE An overabundance of antiques, avidly amassed by this home's owner while he lived in a small city apartment, inspired his move to this creekside cottage. In the bedroom, a white-painted floor and white walls create a crisp backdrop for the black antique iron bed. Color and pattern flow evenly from the head of the bed to the foot, in such hues as white, black, pale pink, and different shades of gray. Elsewhere in the room, solid blocks of white and black provide an anchor for the medley of patterns on the bed.

Conversely, more modern sensibilities can continue their reign by choosing simple patterns and understated furnishings.

Historically, most cottage bedrooms of the late nineteenth and early twentieth centuries were small, and many were tucked right up under the eaves. For this reason, light colors and diminutive patterns on wallpaper and sheets (rosebuds, for example, or thin stripes) were most common. Furnishings, too, were generally pared down to the barest necessities. In the smallest bedrooms you'd often find only a bed, a nightstand, and a dresser. Where space permitted, larger pieces were added: an armoire, a small writing desk and chair, a blanket chest, an armchair and reading lamp. Floors were generally kept bare, with an area rug positioned beside the bed. At the windows, simple lace, eyelet, or sheer curtains did the trick. Decorations on the walls were also kept to a minimum, consisting only of a mirror over the dresser and a single framed painting or print.

More than a century later, this image of the cottage bedroom remains clear in our minds. However, most homeowners today have a bit more space to work with, especially in newer dwellings. Even in period cottages, some owners choose to create a more spacious master suite by combining two smaller bedrooms into

In this guest room, the vintage-inspired wallpaper—bearing a lily-of-the-valley motif—combines with the chenille bedspreads to create a nostalgic, summertime ambience. The scalloped shelf is a classic cottage detail. Ever since the Victorian era, light and airy wicker furniture like the small table seen here has been associated with summer furnishings, perfect for seaside cottages like this one.

one or by adding an extension to the house. Perhaps this increased space explains the shift in our view of the bedroom. Once a place purely for sleep, bedrooms today have taken on new roles: There might be a reading nook near a sunny window, a spot for exercising in front of a television, or a small home office. Fortunately, it's easy to imbue bedrooms of any size with cottage charm.

Paying attention to traditional details—small patterns, light colors, delicate textures, and simple decorations—is the secret to bringing the cottage look to bedrooms of any size, style, and geographic location, be they situated in city apartments, suburban homes, or grand estates. The first area of focus should be the walls: Will you choose paint or wallpaper? Shades of white and creamy pastels are popular choices for paint color, while small-scale flower prints are often used to paper walls in their entirety or sometimes only the space above beaded-board paneling. In some bedrooms, whitewashed paneling is installed floor to ceiling.

The proper bed can set the tone for an entire room, so the question of which style to choose is an important one. Iron beds have an undeniably old-fashioned appeal. Sleigh beds are for true romantics. Upholstered headboards can match curtains or furnishings; the type of fabric can make the room ultrafeminine (a large cabbage-rose print) or more modern (a bold stripe). Trundle beds are great for kids' rooms because they make even the smallest space sleepover-ready. No matter what style of bed frame you choose, bedding should be irresistible: crisp sheets, a pile of soft pillows, and a wonderfully textured quilt or plush duvet.

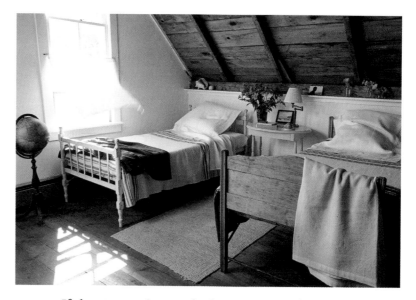

ABOVE Flea-market and thrift-shop finds are perfect for bedrooms in summer cottages where the goal is often to accommodate as many guests as possible with minimum financial expense. White sheets and matching woolen blankets make these mismatched twin bed frames work as a pair. The cheerful yellow bedside table has just enough surface area for a reading lamp, books, and a bouquet of garden flowers. The standing globe adds visual interest and also acts as a conversation piece for guests. The narrow ledge above the beds can be used as display space for tiny vases, family photos, and seashells.

OPPOSITE The "hotel" sign in this spare but elegant bedroom creates a sense of being able to order room service using the old-fashioned rotary telephone on the table. The French iron beds date to the 1930s. The black-painted ceiling beam provides fun contrast to the light-colored walls.

If closet space in your bedroom is not what it should be, additional storage is advisable, not only for clothing but also for extra blankets, stationery, photo albums, or what have you. Armoires are natural choices and can either reveal bare wood or a surface painted to match the room's decor. Imagine a whitewashed armoire against soft-green walls, a polished pine model against a wallpaper pattern of tiny red rosebuds, or a blue-painted cupboard that perfectly matches cheerful blue-and-white gingham sheets.

Because an armoire, on account of its size, can sometimes dominate a bedroom wall, plan displays of art or collections around this piece. For a symmetrical arrangement, hang similarly themed prints (botanical subjects work especially well) on each side. For a more casual look, you might hang three floral plates in a column on one side (using gallery clips) and position three vintage photographs vertically on the other side. The tops of armoires are also great places to display collections like baskets, McCoy vases, or painted wood hat stands. If an armoire is not part of your bedroom plan, cluster artwork over the bed or dresser, or hang a few favorite pieces between windows or doorframes. "Cluster," of course, will mean different things to different people. It may be a row of three gold-framed pansy still lifes in a simply styled lavender room or a collection of half a dozen equine paint-by-numbers over a desk. When choosing art for bedrooms, don't be afraid to look beyond standard forms like paintings, prints, photographs, and drawings. Hooked

OPPOSITE Two beloved collections are on display in this inviting bedroom: landscape paintings featuring idyllic cottage scenes and wind-up clocks that remind the homeowner of her grandmother's treasure-filled cottage in Hungary. White walls and bed linens provide an unobtrusive backdrop for the paintings, thereby allowing the artwork to be shown off to full advantage. The "headboard" is made from a salvaged architectural detail affixed to the wall.

RIGHT Creatively displayed treasures are highly personal finishing touches that make a room special. On this bedside table, a cherished collection of objects, including an elegant white McCoy vase, becomes an evocative still life with a strong visual impact.

rugs with house-and-yard scenes or animal motifs can look great when mounted on the wall, as can baby quilts or trade signs with appropriate themes like "No Vacancy" or "Sweet Dreams Motel."

Window treatments are the finishing touch for any room, and bedrooms are no exception. While many cottage owners choose to leave the windows bare in more public areas of the house, most opt for some type of window covering for privacy here. If the bare or streamlined look appeals to you elsewhere in the house, continue it in the bedroom with white louvered shutters or blinds that can be opened or raised during the day. Another simple style is a half curtain fashioned from lace or sheer fabric in a color that coordinates with other hues in the room. Of course, if your bedroom blooms with exuberant floral prints or other bold patterns, feel free to continue the motif at the window in the form of curtains, drapes, valances, or roman shades.

OPPOSITE LEFT Peaked roofs are typical of many cottages, especially older ones, and the resulting low-ceilinged rooms are best used as bedrooms. The floral wallpaper contrasts nicely with the white ceiling, emphasizing the architecture, and the white nail-edge trunk sits almost at the same height as the window ledge, allowing the maximum amount of light to enter the room. White linens permit the carved bed frames to show off their curves. By hanging light fixtures instead of placing lamps on the trunk, there's plenty of space available for books, a clock, and a small vase of flowers. The plum-colored pillow shams echo the plum floral pattern on the wallpaper.

OPPOSITE RIGHT This restful guest room was created with limited fuss and minimal funds. To color coordinate the space in an instant, walls were painted a soft lavender-blue, a few shades lighter than the prominently placed periwinkle-blue lamp. Because both are white, the mismatched twin bed frames look like a pair. Chenille bedspreads with pom-pom fringes and ticking-stripe pillows on each bed emphasize symmetry. On the wall, two whitewashed wood shelves hung close to each other support a lovely collection of floral-pattern porcelain; the antique mirror adds height to the arrangement. A 1930s hooked rug placed between the beds injects a touch of bold color and pattern to the airy scene.

decorating with plates

Decorative plates look great on the table, but they can also be wonderful solutions to bare walls throughout the house. Group plates by color (brown-and-white transferware or pink lusterware, for example) or theme (such as roses or violets), then center them, smallest (at the top) to largest if they vary in size, over a chair, small desk, or side table to keep the look elegant. Gallery hooks, available at art-supply stores, work well for larger arrangements; ridged art shelves give single plates or short rows of plates an air of importance.

 **RIGHT** With an architectural element as striking as this window, a small bedroom under the eaves needs little else in the way of decoration. Simple furnishings in this room include a graceful iron bed, a small table, and a side chair. Even the floor is unadorned. The blue blanket chest adds a splash of color and provides storage for bedding and guests' belongings as well.

ABOVE Layering collections and furnishings of the same color adds dramatic yet understated texture to a bedroom. In this serene setting, the dresser, hall mirror, and beaded-board paneling have all been whitewashed. Against this backdrop, cherished objects have been carefully arranged: an ironstone footed bowl, a McCoy vase, and a vintage alarm clock.

RIGHT Canopy beds are among the most romantic of furnishings, but the scale of cottage bedrooms sometimes makes them impossible to fit in. A simple drape of sheer or lacy fabric is a wonderful solution, capturing the feeling of a canopy in even the smallest of spaces. A length of fabric and a simple hook or peg are all that are needed to create this look. The graphic floor pattern is an unexpected yet whimsical addition to the room. A similar pattern could be painted onto a wood floor or achieved with common kitchen tiles.

RIGHT One benefit of iron bed frames is that they often can be maneuvered into the tiniest of bedrooms. What's more, their airy quality means that even queen-size frames like this one won't overwhelm a small space. The strong lines of this frame are echoed in the iron curtain rod above the window and the folding stool at the foot of the bed (an item that would make a great luggage rack as well). Wall-to-wall sisal carpeting, butter-yellow walls, plush pillows and quilts, and a reading chair upholstered in white soften the straight lines of the room's metal components. Leaded-glass doors add an elegant touch; search for similar designs at flea markets, salvage shops, and antiques malls.

iron bed frames

A sheer curtain flutters in the breeze by an open window, a transferware ewer and basin rest on a bureau, and an iron bed frame supports
a patchwork quilt and a pile of pillows. These are some of the timeless
images of the cottage bedroom, and central to this mental picture is the
bed frame. Part of the allure of iron bed frames is the range of styles that
can be found, from extremely simple to gracefully curved. The fact
that light and air flow through these frames—as opposed to a mahogany
sleigh bed, for instance—means that you can place one in a very small
bedroom without worrying that it will overpower the space.

The decision facing each cottage decorator with an eye for an iron bed is
whether to buy a new frame, readily available these days through home-
design stores and mail-order sources, or to search for an antique. New
frames often appeal to people because they can offer the old-fashioned
look that's wanted in the exact color and size desired with a minimum of
fuss. This is especially convenient because queen- or king-size frames
can be difficult to find on the antiques market. One drawback to new
frames is that they can be expensive, a fact that leads many people to
scour antiques malls, flea markets, and country auctions in hope of finding a perfect specimen from the past. Most old frames on the market
date from the late nineteenth and early twentieth centuries, when the
style was widely used in summer cottages through the country. Value
will generally depend on age (more recent examples tend to be less
expensive), degree of detail, and painted finish (white is common; soft
blue and green are especially desirable). Although some buyers covet a
well-worn painted finish, many choose to refinish antique frames either
by hand or by hiring a professional furniture restorer. Refinishing is
probably a wise decision if the frame is intended for a child's room, as
most of the paints used years ago were lead-based. A fresh coat of paint
can even make two frames with slightly different designs look like a perfect match—a plus when decorating a child's room or guest room.

quilts

Intricately stitched and beloved by generations, quilts are among the clearest symbols of comfort in American culture, making them a natural choice for the cottage interior. While the pastel palette and romantic pattern names (Grandmother's Flower Garden, Double Wedding Ring, Sunbonnet Sue) of Depression-era quilts complement traditional cottage furnishings particularly well, nearly every design from any age can find a home here. Two-tone creations from the nineteenth century, such as indigo-on-white Flying Geese or red-on-white School House patterns, appear with frequency, as do bold floral appliqués from the 1940s and '50s.

One advantage to twentieth-century quilts is that they tend to be a bit sturdier than delicate nineteenth-century quilts, a plus if you intend to use and display them in a bustling household. New quilts—either from a department store, a boutique, or your own sewing machine—are generally the easiest to care for, as their fabrics are stronger and more colorfast than those used in the past. By and large, new quilts can be popped into the washing machine (gentle cycle, mild detergent) and dryer (low heat) if they get soiled. Many people choose to clean antique and vintage quilts before displaying them directly on beds, sofas, or tabletops. Older quilts should be hand washed, rolled in towels, and laid flat to dry because their stitches and fabrics can become weak or damaged with excessive movement.

Dressing a bed is one of the common ways to display quilts in the cottage home. Bear in mind that if the foot of the bed is a favorite napping area for a family cat or dog, you may want to purchase a coordinating throw or blanket that can be placed over the bottom of the quilt during the day. The habits of house pets should also be taken into account if a quilt is to be displayed over the back of a settee, folded atop a blanket chest, or draped over a wooden quilt rack. Stacking quilts in a cupboard is a wonderful way to showcase favorite designs safely. Although hanging quilts on walls has become popular in recent years, a cottage's size can affect the process. Ideally, quilts hung on a wall should be up off the floor by at least six inches to avoid a buildup of dust. Attractive alternatives for small spaces include mounting crib quilts or quilted wall hangings. Be sure to keep wall-mounted textiles out of direct sunlight, which can cause fading over time.

Whitewashing the walls and rafters of this uninsulated summer cottage created an airy sleeping loft. A portion of picket fence was used to make a one-of-a-kind headboard. Flea-market finds in the room include the small dresser, the hunter-green wicker side table, and the white-washed porch chair. Family photographs and vintage snapshots line the ledge beside the window. An extra quilt folded at the foot of the bed adds color to the all-white space.

OPPOSITE Floral and striped linens in dusty pink hues set against a backdrop of pale green create a cozy atmosphere in this bedroom. The floral theme is continued in the two prints hanging over the dresser, the hatbox (which adds a charming touch of yesteryear while providing useful storage), and the small green vase holding fresh flowers. The curtain rods, with their ball finials, echo the bed's iron frame.

TOP RIGHT Hand-painted furniture was a staple of the Victorian cottage bedroom. Wooden bed frames, small dressers, and bedside tables are among the most common items found in today's antiques markets. This pair of twin beds was made in Austria in the early 1900s. Their new owner crafted matching duvet covers using a coordinating rose-motif fabric she found in a quilt shop. To apply old-fashioned floral motifs to new furniture, consult craft books on stenciling and decorative painting techniques at your local library or bookstore, or search for instructions on the Internet.

BOTTOM RIGHT A paneled bed frame was chosen to echo the whitewashed walls of this sunny bedroom. Bursts of tomato red on the bedside table, armchair, and bedspread set against the sunflower-yellow floor move the eye around the room. Although its scale is smaller than that of the bed, the two-tiered bench is a vital element in the space on account of its usefulness. The area beneath a window is an unexpected yet fun place to hang a painting.

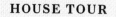
a cottage decorated with antiques

OPPOSITE The bold carpet pattern supplies an anchor for the living room's mixture of furnishings. A sofa piled with pillows, a matching upholstered armchair and ottoman, and a high-back Mission armchair provide plenty of seating.

When two antiques collectors decided they'd had enough of New York City's hectic pace, their search for a country retreat led them to Bucks County, Pennsylvania, a rural oasis only a few hours from the Big Apple. Here, amid rolling hills and quaint villages, the collectors happened upon a 1926 Craftsman-style cottage. Though modest in size, the house featured plenty of windows, original woodwork, and a fireplace surrounded by antique tiles from the Moravian Tile Works in nearby Doylestown, Pennsylvania. It was a perfect match, and the new owners lost no time transforming the interior into a suitable backdrop for their extensive collections of pottery, furniture, textiles, and more.

They turned their attention first to the walls. Instead of wallpaper, the owners chose paint in solid, soft colors that would allow their precious possessions to be the center of attention. For the living room, they chose a warm yellow that took on an extra glow once the room's red, tan, and cream furnishings were put in place. In the dining room, a pale blue was chosen to ground the table, chairs, and accessories painted in deeper shades of red, green, and blue. The kitchen's deep-olive walls and cream woodwork emphasize the intimacy of the small space. The exposed-beam ceilings throughout the first floor were whitewashed to create an open, airy atmosphere.

While color reigns on the first floor of the house, white walls prevail on the second floor, where the bedrooms are kept crisp white, making the cozy quarters tucked under the eaves feel a bit more spacious. White walls also add a sense of serenity to the bedrooms, which are intended very much as respites from the public

OPPOSITE This bright bedroom proves that even the smallest spaces can be turned into charming sanctuaries. Red-and-white vintage linens (including a Robbing Peter to Pay Paul quilt) dress the twin bed. A tiny closet, a few good books, and a single painting and lamp complete the scene.

ABOVE Sage-green shades add a touch of color to the all-white backdrop of this bedroom and complement similar hues seen in the sheets, blankets, and accessories. The leather armchair and stately Mission oak bed frame share the same warm tone. Remnants of a crazy quilt became a cover for the ottoman.

areas of the house. Amplifying the coziness of the upstairs rooms, patchwork quilts and plush pillows dress the beds. Enticing piles of books are arranged on table-tops and, space permitting, inviting armchairs are placed beside sunny windows.

Windows and floors in the house were handled in opposite ways. Windows throughout remain curtainless. Instead, the owners chose shades to keep the line from floor to ceiling clean and unfussy.

Floors were quite another matter: Underfoot, color and pattern were given free reign to run wild over the floorboards. Hooked rugs in classic patterns and flat carpets in bold botanical prints add visual interest to a part of the house that is often overlooked. With the stage set, the owners added their furnishings and collections to the scene.

Although pieces in their collection come from different periods and different geographic regions, their common threads are color and craftsmanship. An appreciation for fine construction has also led the owners to purchase creations by contemporary craftspeople working in traditional methods. New and old, antique and vintage, all items are mixed and matched to create an interior that is a thoroughly livable home, not a museum. As with all successful cottage interiors, comfort is key. Children are always welcome, the owners' two dogs are free to roam, and guests can collapse onto the sofa and put their feet up without a moment's hesitation. The way the owners arrange their collections throughout the cottage is worthy of note as well. First, objects are often removed from the area for which they were originally intended. For instance, late-nineteenth- and early-twentieth-century

RIGHT If these mixing bowls had been relegated to a kitchen shelf, their exquisite colors and patterns would have been far less noticeable. The circa 1900 painted cupboard and the single framed watercolor against the pale-blue wall keep the arrangement's look simple and elegant.

OPPOSITE, TOP LEFT Wood paneling around the fireplace was painted the same shade of yellow as the living room walls. The color complements a collection of Ohio pottery vases and a 1930s flower painting discovered at a flea market. The ceramic deer head on the wall adds a whimsical touch.

OPPOSITE, TOP RIGHT A garden bench stripped of paint now supports books beside a bright window. The leather armchair and upholstered ottoman with flattened ball feet create a cozy spot that invites hours of reading enjoyment.

OPPOSITE, BOTTOM LEFT Butcher-block countertops, old-style iron cabinet hardware, and a hooked rug add country flair to the tiny kitchen. Modern appliances don't seem out of place when kept sleek black below the counters and all white above. Artwork and objects are sparingly arranged.

OPPOSITE, BOTTOM RIGHT New rush-seat chairs and a grandfather clock made from salvaged wood combine with antiques and curios. The circa 1960 hooked rug reflects all the colors found in the room. The shades are affixed to the bottom of the window, letting in sunlight while still providing ample privacy. Tin ornaments were turned into shade pulls at the windows.

mixing bowls are taken out of the kitchen and placed on top of a painted cupboard, allowing guests to focus on (perhaps for the first time) the range of color, pattern, and shape to be found. Elsewhere in the house, a child's toy rests on a kitchen shelf, and a painted workbench supports metal garden ornaments in the dining room. Another tactic is grouping items by theme—size, shape, or color—which effectively increases the visual impact of a collection. This can be seen in the mixing-bowl arrangement, as well as the selection of colorful vases positioned on the mantel. When displayed in unexpected spots or an out-of-the-ordinary manner, cherished objects catch visitors by surprise and bring a smile to their faces.

CHAPTER 4
bathrooms

Bathrooms as we know them today—
separate rooms featuring sink,
toilet, and tub—were a rarity when cottage architecture first reached American shores in the
nineteenth century. Back then, kitchen sinks, copper bathing tubs set beside a fireplace, and outhouses fulfilled a family's various hygienic needs.
As the twentieth century dawned and cottages
became a common style for suburban homes, the
bathroom became a symbol of the modern American lifestyle. Manufacturers of the day began to
design coordinating sinks, tubs, and toilets
appropriate for both grand and modest homes.

Even a bathroom can be a gallery for a collection. Here, a group of wire hangers from the 1920s and '30s makes for interesting and sculptural wall art. The bathroom's marble countertop was formerly a seat from an old bench that was retrofitted for the bathroom. Beaded board topped by a narrow shelf gives the room a classic cottage feel; hooks are user-friendly for hanging towels, bathrobes, and clothing.

SOAPS

OPPOSITE Black-on-white toile wallpaper and a tone-on-tone cushion resting on a side chair add a modern freshness to the old-fashioned features of this bathroom, namely the antique mirror, claw-foot tub, peg rail, and paneling. Toiletries are stored in ticking-stripe bags suspended from the peg rail.

While outhouses would remain common sights at vacation cottages well into the 1900s, no town residence was considered fashionable without a distinct bathroom.

From the start, homeowners began beautifying this utilitarian room. Women's magazines offered ideas for pretty curtains, wall stencil patterns, hooked rugs, and framed prints and photographs. Even today, bathroom remodeling articles are among the most popular features in home-design magazines. Perhaps the small size of the room lets homeowners feel free to experiment with colors and patterns they might consider too bold for other rooms in the house. There are so many ways to approach decorating the cottage bathroom. One of the most classically old-fashioned looks involves beaded-board paneling on the bottom half of the walls with soft pastel paint or wallpaper bearing a tiny floral print above. Ideal accessories for such a room include a claw-foot tub, a pedestal sink, and wispy curtains made of eyelet or gingham. A darker, more Victorian feeling could be created with hunter-green walls and matching curtains and sink skirt fashioned from a strong pink-and-green rose fabric. Even a sleekly modern bathroom in light colors with marble floors, glass shelves, and plenty of chrome fixtures can work in today's cottage home.

In sharp contrast to generations past, a spa atmosphere is highly desirable in home bathrooms today. Larger pieces like whirlpool tubs may pose a challenge to anyone who has a small space to work with, but more compact details such as wall-mounted towel warmers and clear-glass shower stalls can be incorporated into any size bathroom. Depending on how strongly you want certain features, you

Narrow bathrooms can be made spectacular with grand details such as a vaulted ceiling and a graceful footed sink. Stainless-steel fixtures and accessories throughout the space look especially sleek when set against an all-white backdrop. Wall-mounted makeup or shaving mirrors are elegant amenities that can be added to large or small bathrooms. Windowsills are ideal spots for displaying collections of glass; the play of sunlight through clear or colored jars, bottles, and bowls can be stunning. A pair of salvaged balusters finds a new home flanking the window and now serves as an attractive frame for the garden view.

might consider increasing the square footage of your bathroom by removing either a closet or a wall nearby. But even if you choose to work within the confines of the room's original layout, remember that cottage charm can be achieved around the most modern of fixtures with the use of vintage details like beaded-board paneling, old-fashioned tile patterns, and pedestal sinks.

Before beginning a bathroom makeover, assess the room's basics. Are the sink, tub, and toilet in good condition and of a style that you like? If an old home retains its claw-foot tub or pedestal sink, are they free from chips and discoloration? If not, they may need to be resurfaced by a plumber or bathroom specialist. Unless a complete overhaul is called for, most bathroom remodelings leave existing fixtures in place. If your home features 1960s- or '70s-era sinks and toilets in colors you're not crazy about (avocado green, perhaps, or sunflower yellow), consider wall treatments that might tone down the retro look before deciding to gut the room. For instance, yellow bathroom furnishings could look lovely in a room with whitewashed beaded board up half the wall and wallpaper featuring thin yellow and white stripes above. Likewise, imagine avocado fixtures in an all-white room with green-and-white gingham curtains, green towels, and a pot of trailing ivy on a shelf above a window.

Using beaded-board paneling or tiles halfway up the walls leaves the top of the walls free for paint or wallpaper. Although all-white is an enduring look for cottage bathrooms, some people choose to experiment with stronger paint shades (sky blue, apple green, or caramel brown) or more graphic wallpaper patterns (checks,

stripes, or florals) precisely because the wall space here is limited. On the floors, small tile patterns are most common. Daring souls might try larger tiles, checkerboard patterns, or a solid color in an otherwise all-white room (like ocean blue or sea-foam green). Rugs add warmth underfoot when placed in front of the sink or beside the tub or shower; solid colors can coordinate with a curtain fabric or wallpaper pattern while hooked or woven rugs can add a nostalgic touch to the room.

Storage is an important consideration in cottage bathrooms, especially when undersink cabinets or linen closets are not large enough. If you have a freestanding sink whose base you do not mind covering up, a sink skirt can create ample hidden storage with minimal fuss. Simply choose a fabric that coordinates with the colors or patterns already found in the room, then hem all sides and stitch one side of Velcro tape to the top, facing front. Using epoxy glue, attach the other side of Velcro to the inside top of the sink, then press the two parts together. Baskets are another quick, attractive way to expand storage space in the bathroom. Magazines, towels, washcloths, and extra rolls of toilet paper can all be stylishly stored here. Even chairs, stools, and narrow plant stands can become additional bathroom storage. Set beside the tub or window, they can gracefully support stacks of towels or wire baskets filled with toiletries. Where space allows, consider a hutch, bookcase, or small cupboard originally intended for other rooms in the house. A fresh coat of white paint (or a shade that coordinates well with the room) will help these furnishings blend into their new surroundings.

RIGHT Vanity tables are desirable amenities, but many cottage home-owners think the table-and-chair sets cannot fit into small rooms. As this photograph illustrates, however, even modest bathrooms can accommodate vanities if they are well designed. A shallow but serviceable ledge with drawers, cabinets, and space for a diminutive wooden stool was planned along one wall of this sunny bath. A mirror was positioned between the windows; a lamp hung above the mirror provides additional lighting for makeup applications. Sea-green floor tiles add a dash of color to the all-white room.

To decorate bathroom walls, choose works of art that will not be damaged by humidity and occasional splashes of water. Framed botanical prints can be a nice look here, as can framed Victorian advertisements for soaps, tooth powders, and face creams. Seashore motifs work particularly well in the bath, so feel free to frame vintage engravings of seashells or watercolors of coastal scenes. To empha-size a room's overall theme, coordinate collections with art—seashells and beach glass in a room with nautical art, for example, or a selection of nineteenth-century cold-cream jars beneath Victorian beauty advertisements.

OPPOSITE LEFT **Although space is limited, pattern and texture abound in this bathroom. Striped wallpaper, beaded-board paneling, an embroidered curtain, a checkerboard floor pattern, and a stenciled pattern on the bathtub coexist peacefully because all share a neutral color scheme.**
OPPOSITE RIGHT **To add color and texture to the bathroom, one crafty homeowner transformed a chenille bedspread into a shower curtain. Cotton camp blankets, colorful quilt tops, and graphic bark cloth would also work well for this purpose. Before hanging, hem all sides of the fabric and reinforce the holes along the top with grommets. Choose a coordinating shower-curtain liner in clear, white, or colored vinyl to protect the fabric from splashing water.**

decorating with chandeliers

Chandeliers can add a whimsical touch when hung in a casual or unexpected setting, such as a bathroom. Although glimmering crystal is not unheard of in a cottage, more classic designs include painted toleware in a floral motif, Scandinavian-style ironwork, and graceful brass with cloth shades. Many old chandeliers can be electrified and antique lamps rewired. Turn to page 123 for a beautiful blue and white bathroom sporting a vintage chandelier.

beaded board

The ability of beaded board to create a look that is at once clean-lined and textured is one reason this narrow-striped wood paneling has enjoyed such lasting appeal. Another benefit is beaded board's myriad uses throughout the house: It can be applied to walls, it can cover the outside of large furnishings like cupboards and kitchen work islands, and it can be used to construct small chests for blankets, board games, and toys. Because it is easy to clean and has a distinctly casual personality, beaded board is found most frequently in kitchens and bathrooms. It is most commonly used to coat walls—sometimes up to waist height and sometimes to within a foot or two of the ceiling. Opting for near-ceiling height is a good way to keep a strong paint color or bold wallpaper pattern from overpowering a room.

Even waist-high beaded board will help break up a large expanse of wall, letting homeowners use color and pattern freely without worrying about how a full wall will look coated in robin's-egg blue or apple green, or papered with a rose-trellis print. Most often, beaded board is painted white, but that shouldn't stop you from experimenting with other colors. In all-white settings, beaded board can become a source of contrast in the room when painted a deeper shade of off-white or tan or perhaps a brighter hue such as blue, green, or lavender.

Carpenters and contractors will be able to install beaded board in your home. To try your hand at the process, visit a local home-improvement store to purchase the paneling and receive installation advice. For most room projects, purchasing a complementary molding to place around the top of the beaded board is advisable because it gives the paneling a more finished look. Bring the dimensions of the walls along which you want the beaded board to go (measure both the length of the wall and the height you want the beaded board to reach). Snapshots of the space will also help store personnel assist you in choosing the best style for the room.

RIGHT Beaded board coats the walls, floor to ceiling, in this bathroom. Keeping the walls white and painting the ceiling a soft green is a fun use of color. Beaded board also covers the bottom shelf of a long wood table into which his-and-her basins have been set. A wicker magazine holder is ideal for hand towels; wire baskets can hold decorative items (dried starfish are seen here) or practical ones (such as bath sponges or washcloths). On top of the table, glass canisters and apothecary jars hold bars of soap and cotton balls. A striking image like the rhododendron painting hung between the medicine cabinets can be all a small room needs on its walls.

ABOVE Glass display cases are wonderful places to store towels and toiletries. Not only will the case's contents be protected from dust, they can be artfully arranged to add visual interest to the room. Wire baskets like the one set on top of the display case can hold extra rolls of toilet paper in style. Botanical prints were natural choices for the walls; the green frames stand out against the blue walls in a pleasing manner.

RIGHT Using two tones of the same color in a single setting is an easy way to create a decorator-perfect space. In this bath, a dramatic sink table has been painted a deep periwinkle blue while the walls above the white tiles wear a significantly lighter shade. To better match the proportions of the table, the medicine cabinet was set into a larger frame. With all the color choices in stores these days, towels can become decorative accessories in the bathroom. Choose a single shade that matches the walls or shower curtain in your bath, or select a range of colors like the white, lavender, light-blue, and deep-plum towels displayed here.

RIGHT Iridescent glass tile on the tub surround, horizontal wainscoting on the walls, and aged limestone-like ceramic tile on the floor—this mix of materials creates an inviting ambience that's perfect for the master bath in a lakeside home. The vintage table, decorated with seashells, continues the water theme that appears throughout the house while adding one-of-a-kind charm to the space.

antique sinks

Your bathroom can be new from floor to ceiling—sparkling white tiles, delicately striped wallpaper, gleaming brass towel holders—yet if you install an antique sink, the room will instantly radiate an authentic old-fashioned aura. No wonder these items are so eagerly sought by decorators, collectors, and restoration experts. Ask any architectural salvage source or antiques shop in your area, and they'll tell you that antique sinks are hot commodities, and when they appear, they're snapped up quickly. But don't despair; these fixtures appear on the market regularly, so you won't have to wait too long to find your perfect match. Examples from the not-too-distant past (the 1930s and '40s) are showing up with greater frequency these days and generally cost less than late-nineteenth- and early-twentieth-century models.

Many styles of sinks can work in the cottage bathroom. The most classic is the pedestal sink. Within this style are numerous variations, from extremely sleek designs to those that are more curvaceous. The style you choose will likely depend on the other details of the room. Curving forms will complement more romantic takes on the bathroom; sleek sinks will fit a modern decor. Another good choice for a more contemporary vision of the cottage bath is a deep double sink, originally found in kitchens and laundry rooms. These can be a fun change from the standard his-and-her sinks.

To find the sink of your dreams, scour architectural salvage stores, antiques shops, or flea markets. Antique sinks even appear on Web auctions from time to time. If you don't see the exact style you want right away, show dealers a picture of what you're looking for and ask them to keep an eye out for you. Many will be interested in the offer, will take your number, and will call you if and when they find a match.

With all antique bathroom items—sinks, tubs, toilets—chances are good that you'll need to resurface the porcelain and replace the fittings. Fortunately, a number of companies make plumbing fixtures based on antique designs, and many sell directly through nationwide home-improvement stores. Enlist the aid of a plumber or general contractor to return your piece to its original glory.

a French country cottage

OPPOSITE To make her small bedroom appear larger, the owner positioned a large antique French mirror as a grand headboard. From time to time, the bed's quilts get rotated with others from her collection to subtly alter the look of the room.

Inspiration for decorating comes in many forms. Some people take cues from a cherished collection or from a favorite era of design. A love of French country style was the driving force for the owner of this California cottage. Every room in the charming 1930s dwelling is imbued with the colors and spirit of French country—with a decidedly American flair. When the owner first spied the cottage, she questioned whether the 1,600-square-foot space would feel crowded once her furniture and collections were in place. Quite the opposite has been true. Light-colored walls, abundant sunlight, and a unifying color scheme have created an interior that is exuberant without being overpowering.

To make the cozy floor plan appear roomier, neutral colors from eggshell to palest lemon were used throughout the house. On walls, light colors like these reflect sunlight, visually expanding a small space. Against this backdrop, the owner layered her furniture—mainly French country and American antiques—with many items upholstered or embellished with her extensive fabric collection. Choosing red as the dominant color allowed the owner to combine numerous prints into a harmonious look. The dining room, for example, is a lively mix of checks, stripes, and florals—some seven patterns in all from the flowery rug to the upholstered chairs to the draperies.

OPPOSITE Different patterns were used for the front and back of the dining room chairs. Placing the table at an angle adds interest to the small space. Red-and-white plaid was used as trim on one set of drapes, and as valances on the others.

RIGHT Stripes, checks, florals, and toiles combine in the living room's energetic mix. The black background of two throw pillows is reflected in the lampshade at the far end of the sofa. The marble-topped French coffee table dates to the eighteenth century.

Throughout the house, gleaming wood floors are dressed with ornately patterned rugs. Each design is different, yet all feature light colors and a profusion of flowers, which adds visual interest to rooms without weighing down the overall look. Window treatments vary from flowing drapes to completely bare, to match the mood and purpose of the room. The master bedroom's red-and-white toile drapes are a perfect counterpart to the room's toile and floral prints, while a wide, sunny window seat in the living room is left unadorned.

As the proprietor of a fine-jewelry store, the owner has a knack for combining objects into striking vignettes. She selects a few objects, usually one with height, such as a lamp or vase, and surrounds it with a few others that display an eye-catching color, texture, or antique finish—a pretty plate, a bowl of fruit, an old book.

As a finishing touch in any home, the owner has one last bit of unconventional design advice: add a touch of mustard yellow to every room. Look carefully and you'll spot these elements in each room in her cottage. There's a toleware bowl holding flowers on a table beside the sofa, a lovely antique cupboard in the dining room, and a floral still life in the bedroom. "Whatever your color scheme," she declares, "every room needs a bit of mustard yellow to make it feel sunny."

OPPOSITE Departing from the cottage's dominant color scheme, the bathroom features blue-and-white fabrics and a custom-designed seashell border. Shell-encrusted accessories in the room include the chandelier and the small vases on the windowsill. A small seascape rests beside the tub. RIGHT Just outside the front door, decorative ironwork was added to the cottage's white posts. The simple arrangement of a pretty mirror, a small cupboard, and an eye-catching lamp makes a statement as soon as guests enter the house.

CHAPTER 5
details

PREVIOUS PAGE Wicker porch furniture is a cottage classic. To achieve maximum flexibility, the owners used the same green-and-white fabrics for both indoor and outdoor living spaces, thereby allowing chairs and cushions to be shuffled easily between the two areas.

Two cottage rooms may be similar in many ways: They may both have white walls, white slipcovered furnishings, and whitewashed shutters on the windows. What will set them apart, however, will be the collections, the artwork, and the countless details that personalize a home and mark it, unmistakably, as the dwelling of its owner. Imagine that one homeowner were an avid gardener. She might place miniature topiaries along the mantel in her all-white room, hang framed botanical prints above the sofa, and lay a floral-motif hooked rug underfoot. A collector of contemporary glass, on

PREVIOUS PAGE Several techniques for displaying collections can be found in this photograph. In the kitchen, a cupboard has been designated the showcase for a lively group of enamelware coffee- and teapots. Choosing just a few for each shelf highlights the subtleties of each design. The wall space above a doorway is a great place to hang long, narrow items such as the train depot sign shown here; panoramic photographs and vintage vacation banners would also work well. Plates hung on the wall in the dining area create a pleasing (and space-appropriate) arrangement.

the other hand, might line her mantel with colorful Murano vases; opt for playful watercolors in bright blues, yellows, and reds on the walls; and choose a royal-blue carpet for the floor. Though the backgrounds in each room are the same, the end results are as different as can be. Once you've covered the basics in your home, here are some distinguishing details to consider.

Displaying Collections

The objects we choose to surround ourselves with say a lot about who we are, revealing clues to our pastimes and passions. Arranged in the home, collections not only help visitors understand their hosts a little better, they often spark conversations. When collections grow large, as they are wont to do, it's not always easy to determine where to put them or how to pare them down. There's a tendency to want to show everything at once, when selecting a few favorite pieces—and rotating others in and out of the arrangement—might make a greater visual impact. For sizable collections, it can be helpful to designate an area just for them, like a cupboard, curio cabinet, or bookcase. Large collections can also be displayed in small clusters around the house: A person with an eye for roses, for example, might fill a dining room cupboard with rose-pattern china, line a living room shelf with rose still lifes, and hang a row of vintage hats brimming with silk roses from a peg rail in the bedroom or foyer.

OPPOSITE Emptying a few shelves in a bookcase creates an ideal place to display prized possessions. When positioning fragile pieces, such as this collection of pink lusterware, clear away all the books and devote the entire shelf to the collection. Sturdier objects such as cast-iron doorstops, on the other hand, can share shelf space with books without much fear that a leaning volume will cause significant damage.

RIGHT There are many advantages to displaying collections along a high shelf. For one thing, fragile or valuable items can be kept out of reach of pets and curious hands. Second, a single long row highlights subtle differences between objects. Finally, the shelf and its contents become an eye-catching wall decoration in the room.

RIGHT Entryways can easily become cluttered with shoes, bags, hats, and anything else that's easy to drop at the door. Here, baskets fitted to small cubbies store umbrellas, sunscreen, and other items. A Shaker-style peg rail adds character and utility, perfect for hanging up gear and keeping the bench clear for sitting. The palette of soft greens and blues contrasts beautifully with the white walls.

OPPOSITE Custom-built cubbies with space for baskets and peg rails are especially good for mudrooms and entryways. Store umbrellas, hats, and scarves in the baskets. A large cubby in the center can be used as a seat for changing muddy boots or sandy flip-flops. A similar wall unit would also be a welcome addition in a laundry room (to house an iron, detergent, spray starch, and other items) or a kid's room (to organize toys, clothes, and childhood sundries).

Storage Solutions

Many cottage homes lack ample storage for collections and everyday items. Wire-rack systems (available at home-improvement stores) and other organizers help make use of every inch of space in closets and cabinets. When closet space is exhausted, creative solutions can be devised throughout the house. Armoires can be transformed into entertainment centers in living rooms and dens, into extra closets in bedrooms, and into pantries for dry goods and glassware in kitchens. Baskets are another attractive alternative: In the living room they can hold firewood, magazines, or warm throws; in the bedroom, extra blankets, sewing supplies, or favorite novels; in the bathroom, towels, washcloths, and toiletries. Selecting furnishings that serve dual purposes can also be a big help: A blanket chest positioned in front of a sofa, for example, becomes both coffee table and additional storage for board games, DVDs, and photo albums.

ABOVE When cottage bedrooms lack ample storage space, armoires prove extremely useful. In addition to storing clothing and extra blankets, they can artfully hide televisions and stereos. When painted the same color as the walls (here it's white on white), even large pieces can blend seamlessly into the closest of quarters.

RIGHT Roomy cupboards with wonderful painted finishes are eagerly sought for cottage homes. Once a large cupboard has reached its full storage capacity, a collection of baskets in various shapes and sizes can be used to accommodate additional objects. Single wooden side chairs and small tables are common sights at flea markets; paired together in a setting like this—where each piece of furniture has a style all its own— makes even mismatched items seem like a perfect fit.

cupboards

The perfect cupboard, prominently positioned, can instantly impart cottage style to any room in the house. Of course, the exact size, style, and color of each person's "perfect" cupboard will vary greatly. Fortunately, countless designs have developed over the years to accommodate almost every taste.

Perhaps your ideal design is a blue-painted pie cupboard from the 1800s that you discovered in an antiques shop. Or maybe it's a sturdy pine hutch with open shelves above and a spacious cabinet below that you spotted in a catalogue. You may have inherited your grandmother's 1930s mahogany breakfront as part of her dining room set. If unsure of your ideal match, browse through decorating magazines and home-design books for inspiration.

Once you've found your heart's desire, the next step will be deciding where to place it and what items to store in it. The dining room has always been the most common location for large, freestanding cupboards. In the nineteenth and early twentieth centuries, they served as both storage and display space for a family's everyday wares and precious heirlooms: pottery, glassware, pewter, and the like.

Breaking with tradition, cupboards originally intended for the dining room have also been making appearances in other parts of the house. In the living room pictured here, for instance, an antique corner cupboard not only protects a few artfully placed possessions, it adds a burst of color to the room as well. A cupboard featuring glass doors on its upper half could be placed in a bedroom where it might hold silver-framed family photographs on the visible shelves above and warm blankets in the hidden storage space provided by the cabinet below; in the bathroom, it could be towels and washcloths above and bars of soap, rolls of toilet tissue, and cleaning supplies below. Although many designs are attractive exactly as they are, some people enjoy embellishing cupboards with decorative treatments such as patterned drawer liners or scalloped paper edging along the end of each shelf. Decals or stenciled designs can be applied to cupboard doors, a popular option when the furnishings are used in children's rooms. Applying wallpaper in a pretty floral print to the interior of a solid-door cupboard presents a lovely surprise each time you go to retrieve a plate, platter, or whatever you may have stored inside.

Flea-market decorating is an easy way to fill your home with one-of-a-kind items that express your passions. The gardening enthusiast who lives in this cottage keeps a weather eye for outdoor items appropriate for indoor use when browsing through the offerings at flea markets. Porch and patio furniture populate these rooms; a fresh coat of hunter-green paint was used to unify different chair designs. Gathering baskets set on top of the armoire add a rustic texture and provide extra storage space as well. Other nature-inspired accessories include the green vases, botanical print, and faux-bamboo frame.

Flea-Market Style

Flea markets are great places to uncover collectibles, storage units, and one-of-a-kind furnishings for the home—nearly all at bargain prices, making these sales ideal for anyone decorating on a budget. The secret to successful flea-market decorating is learning to spot potential when perusing a sale. Anyone who's been to a flea market even once knows that the furniture and accessories found there are rarely in perfect condition. More often than not they have a slight scuff here and there, or they are missing a leg or a drawer pull. If you can train your eye to see the graceful curves hidden beneath layers of unattractive paint, you'll master this style of decorating in no time. Add to this the ability to think up new uses for old objects (cobblers' benches as coffee tables, medicine bottles as bud vases, for example), and you're home free. Having a single color scheme to search for can also make flea-market shopping a bit easier: If you know you're looking for only white wares—or items that can easily be whitewashed—you can keep an eye out for just those things and overlook much of the jumble found at these sources.

ABOVE Displayed on the wall, a small section of wrought-iron fencing becomes a piece of sculpture. The salvaged garden element is especially fitting in this setting, where a patio table has been positioned beside a chaise longue, and fresh flowers abound. Many styles of fencing can be found to fit just about any decor, from highly ornamental to sleek and modern.

RIGHT Removing nonstructural walls created a single large room that incorporates living, dining, and cooking areas. White walls, woodwork, and furnishings create a cohesive look throughout. Items originally intended for outdoor use look great in cottage interiors: Here, garden chairs surround the dinner table, sap buckets hold potted plants on the mantel, and a cement urn stores firewood by the hearth.

Garden Elements

Just as fresh flowers brighten a room, furnishings and accessories originally intended for the garden establish a connection with the great outdoors. Wicker porch furniture, sundials, fruit baskets, and blown-glass cloches are just a few examples of garden elements that can be used in the home. Decorating with these pieces might be as subtle as placing diminutive terra-cotta flowerpots on your desk to hold pens and paper clips or as eye-catching as positioning a set of vintage patio chairs around the dining table. Incorporate a cement cupid bearing remnants of moss into a botanical centerpiece for a dinner party, decoupage a storage box with colorful seed packets, or hang a portion of ornate wrought-iron fencing on the wall as a work of art. Removed from their traditional settings and displayed on a mantel or shelf, antique watering cans, garden tools, and other objects can be appreciated for their sculptural qualities and weathered patinas. Flea markets, antiques shops, and nurseries are good places to search for garden elements both old and new.

RIGHT There are two ways to incorporate architectural elements into the cottage interior: Place them where they were originally intended (a stained-glass transom above a front door, for example) or invent a new use (a stained-glass transom hung on the wall as a work of art). Here, a weathered architectural element (an exterior window frame in its former life, perhaps) serves as part of a table-top composition.

OPPOSITE Although salvaged windows are great for cabinet doors, as seen in this airy, light-filled kitchen, finding large numbers of matching windows can be difficult. Let dealers or salvage sources know what you are searching for; most will keep an eye out for specific designs and call when they locate them.

Architectural Salvage

Materials removed from old houses slated for demolition can be used in two different ways when it comes to cottage decorating. The first is to employ them for practical purposes. Wide-plank pine flooring, elegant mantels, kitchen cabinetry, pedestal sinks, and other items are ideal for renovations or new constructions where period authenticity is desired. The second is to incorporate salvaged elements as purely decorative accents. A stained-glass window hung on the wall can be as pleasing as any painting; a bowl filled with amethyst-glass doorknobs on the coffee table is sure to spark lively conversation. With a creative eye, old architectural details can even be reborn as entirely new items. Glue felt squares to the bottom of ceramic tiles to make attractive coasters, mount mirrors onto squares of tin ceiling tile, or position a section of picket fencing behind a bed for a unique headboard. The possibilities are as endless as the number of objects you'll find in a salvage shop. Check your local yellow pages or conduct a Web search for salvage sources in your area. Bring dimensions with you, especially if you are looking for a large item or for building materials.

RIGHT Porches can be decorated like any other room in the house: They can be filled with the furnishings, collections, and accessories you love most. They can also be given a pared-down look or a style that is over-the-top. This owner's passion for red and green is evident in the red geraniums, the fabrics cushioning the wicker settees, the wire birdcage, and the transferware plates on the porch post. A sunshade held in place with plaid ribbon can be let down on bright afternoons.

OPPOSITE The owner of this 1880s cedar-shingled cottage renovated every square inch of the house, including the spacious wraparound porch, with its unusual green vaulted ceiling. Red is used as an accent color here, appearing on the table lamp and on the assortment of welcoming cushions on the white wicker settee and chair.

Porches

Over the years, these outdoor "rooms" have become some of the most beloved spots in the cottage home, and their decoration often receives the same level of attention as the rest of the house. Floorboards are lovingly painted; chairs and cushion fabrics carefully chosen; and hanging flower baskets lushly planted. Porch furnishings vary in style and include ornate wicker settees, rustic bent-twig rockers, and wrought-iron tables with gleaming glass tops. Front porches should always be ready to welcome friends, family, and first-time visitors. An uncluttered look—a pair of comfortable rockers and a small table on which to rest cool drinks, for example—works best here. Because a back or side porch tends to be more private, this is the place for hammocks, picnic tables, baskets filled with board games, and items of a personal nature. If the design of your porch (and the size of your budget) allows, it might be worth considering glass windows that can enclose the space in the winter, making the porch a room you can use year-round.

OPPOSITE A front or side porch doesn't need much to be cheerful and welcoming. Folding chairs are good items to keep on hand; these versatile seats can be brought out when visitors arrive and can be easily stored when not in use. Here, a glossy coat of barely blue paint enlivens the floor, steps, and ceiling. A potted hydrangea and a climbing rose blur the line between garden and porch, enhancing both.

RIGHT Daybeds are great porch accessories, handy for both lively gatherings and restful afternoon naps. A trundle provides storage for toys, magazines, and other items. On screened porches, daybeds can even be used for outdoor sleeping on warm nights. A collection of vintage-fabric pillows in reds and greens complements the soft green of the bed frame.

RIGHT Colorful blooms and garden furnishings, such as a painted bench, rooster-and-hen statuary, a bee skep, and porch chairs, populate this cheerful garden. Trellises (available at home-improvement stores) are iconic cottage elements, especially when climbing roses, morning glories, or other flowering vines are allowed to thrive. The peg rail hung beside the door displays a Frisbee and a collection of vintage buoys, but would be equally useful for dog leashes, garden hats, and light jackets.

cottage gardens

As long as there have been cottages, there have been cottage gardens—plots that exude the same carefree, irreverent style as the rooms within. Historically, a cottage's front garden would have featured a straight path leading from the street to the front door, flanked on both sides by exuberant plantings of old-fashioned flowers—phlox, hollyhocks, daisies, delphiniums, foxgloves. Garden plots at the back of the house often incorporated herbs and vegetables, bee skeps, chicken coops, fruit trees, and storage sheds. Today most cottage gardens—both front and back—resemble the front gardens of old: Heavy hydrangea blossoms add bursts of blue, pink, and white; climbing roses adorn trellises and porch columns; and fragrant lavender and cheerful daisies line winding brick paths. Books about cottage gardens will help you determine what plant and flower varieties grow best in your region of the country. Dozens of volumes have been written on the subject.

Like any room in the cottage home, cottage gardens are generally outfitted with "furnishings" all their own. Wrought-iron garden benches or rustic bent-twig table-and-chair sets, for example, are commonly placed amid the greenery, providing a quiet spot to meditate in the afternoon. Trellises and arbors are essential elements as well, providing an ideal home for climbing roses. Birdhouses and garden statuary, such as cement turtles or bronze bunnies, add a whimsical touch to the scene. To infuse your yard with instant old-fashioned flavor, seek out vintage garden accessories such as birdhouses, trellises, and garden benches at flea markets and garden-antiques shows. Although chicken coops and bee skeps are rare sights in most gardens today, small wooden structures that can double as a storage facility and potting shed are popular and can be found through home-improvement stores. Painted sheds—red with white trim or white with black trim, for instance—look especially charming in the cottage garden.

City dwellers need not lament their lack of acreage: The spirit of a cottage garden can dwell on a small terrace, in a window box, even along a sunny windowsill. Potted flowers and herbs, rustic birdhouses, and small trellises can be called upon in these situations. In addition to consulting a book on cottage gardens, peruse a volume on indoor gardening or potted gardens to discover which classic cottage blooms will thrive indoors or in small containers.

small cottage, big style

OPPOSITE When decorating the living room, the owners updated the look of classic English country interiors (rooms filled with antiques, over-stuffed furniture, botanical patterns, and framed prints) with a green-and-brown color scheme and their own sense of style.

Imagine the ultimate decorating challenge and it might be this: Transform a former schoolhouse with only 900 square feet of space (small even by cottage standards) into a welcoming home brimming with vibrant colors and patterns. That's just what the owners of this nineteenth-century gem were faced with when they purchased it. Located in New York's Catskill region, the cottage had been neglected for years. Burst pipes and layers of old wallpaper and paint had left the structure in poor condition to say the least. The first step was a complete gut renovation that would allow the couple to start from scratch.

With a clean slate to work with, the next step was devising a floor plan that would best utilize the limited space. The owners decided to divide the first floor into a living area in the front of the house and a kitchen/dining area in the back. In the center of the house are a staircase and a small foyer. Some might feel that devoting precious space to a foyer was an indulgence that cost the owners more living space; their viewpoint was that this architectural element more often associated with larger homes would lend their small abode an air of grandeur. Charming bedrooms tucked under the eaves and a pretty bathroom are found upstairs.

Storage was an issue from the beginning, since the cottage did not have a single closet before the renovation. The solution was to build cupboards, drawers, and bookshelves into the sides of the bedrooms, where the eaves are so low it is impossible to stand up. A secretary in the living room and a tall hutch in the kitchen also hold collections and necessities in style. It helps that the cottage is a weekend retreat, allowing the owners to pare down the pieces they keep here to a minimum.

OPPOSITE Vintage state plates adorn one wall of the kitchen/dining area. Tile floors, stainless-steel appliances, and black cabinetry topped with white marble add a modern flair to the cottage. Meanwhile, a yellow wisteria print gracing the seat cushions and overhead light provides a softening touch.

ABOVE LEFT Chocolate brown is the ideal background for antique prints like the equestrian images in this bedroom. The brown hue is mirrored in the graphic cover of the daybed. Providing a sense of unity, the green-and-white throw pillows continue the color scheme from downstairs.

ABOVE RIGHT A sunny yellow door and a green railing offer a hint of the color scheme to be found inside the circa 1840 dwelling. Matching lantern-style outdoor lights flank the front and side doors of the white clapboard house.

Nevertheless, ample storage space is key in any home to prevent a cluttered look—clutter can make even the roomiest interiors feel cramped.

Regarding the decoration of the rooms, the owners chose to be as adventurous with color and pattern as they would have been in the grandest of homes. In their words, "In a small house such as ours, color works to expand the horizons of what might otherwise be seen as just a really tight space." The use of bold prints and vivid colors keeps the focus away from the actual dimensions of the cottage. Green is the dominant color throughout, with dashes of yellow here and there to brighten the mix. Their advice for combining graphic fabrics in a room is to limit large-scale prints to no more than two, and keep other patterns geometric.

A final word to avid collectors who might be faced with similarly limited square footage. Take a page from these owners' notebook and choose collections that can be displayed on the wall—such as the vintage state plates in the kitchen or the antique prints that grace the bedroom walls. Arrangements such as these have all the vitality that an abundant tabletop collection possesses without sacrificing living space.

OPPOSITE In the master bedroom, dashes of pink pop against a backdrop of cheerful yellow paint. Yellow piping on the head- and footboard's leaf-and-vine print echoes the color of the walls. Bookcases built beneath the eaves keep favorite titles close at hand.
RIGHT The home's low-pitched roof created a seemingly unusable three-foot-high gap on both sides of the master bedroom. The homeowners hired a carpenter to build cabinets and storage drawers on one side—which helped compensate for the lack of closets in the home—and bookshelves on the other side (shown on the opposite page).

CHAPTER 6

instant cottage

Following are twenty-five decorating ideas that can be executed quickly—some take a minute, some an hour, some an afternoon—to instill any home with instant cottage character and charm.

CLOCKWISE FROM TOP LEFT Dress a table with a vintage tablecloth. Arrange fresh flowers in an everyday pitcher. Use straw hats as decorative elements in the house. Make pillows out of vintage tablecloths.
OPPOSITE Top a bedside table with a decorative-edged doily.

CLOCKWISE FROM TOP LEFT Line linen closet shelves with delicate paper edging. Keep bars of soap in a milk-glass compote in the bathroom. Keep a picnic basket close at hand for impromptu outings. Use large baskets to store extra quilts, pillows, or warm throws.

TOP Hang a hooked rug on the wall.
BOTTOM Mount a hand-painted trade sign on the wall.

FOR RENT
2 Bed Room Cottage
WITH
FURNISHED KITCHEN
BY NIGHT OR WEEK

TOP Trim the tops of windows with lace valances.
BOTTOM Install a high shelf above the windows to use for storage and display.

CLOCKWISE FROM TOP LEFT Line a ledge with vintage photographs. Paint a staircase. Place baskets in cubbies to store napkins, flatware, and other household goods. Attach a fabric skirt to the kitchen or bathroom sink.

CLOCKWISE FROM TOP LEFT Transform canning jars into flower vases. Paint a checkerboard pattern on the floor. Use vintage picnic tins as storage for dry goods, napkins, and other kitchenware. Lay a classic country rug on the floor.

CLOCKWISE FROM TOP LEFT Add a decorative trim to shelves. Store plates in an open rack in the kitchen. Install rounded corner shelves to display favorite collections. Arrange antique watering cans along a bench or shelf.

photography credits

Lucas Allen: 42 & 43, 45, 84 (left), 145, 146, 147, 148, 149

Andre Baranowski: 143 (top)

Pierre Chanteau: 90 (bottom)

Jonn Coolidge: 33 (bottom), 37, 38, 40, 41, 110, 119, 120, 121, 122, 123, 156 (top left, bottom right)

Grey Crawford: 156 (top right)

Richard Felber: 25

Gridley & Graves: 33 (top), 83, 95, 96, 97, 98, 99, 128, 132 (right), 142, 154 (top), 157 (top right)

iStock: Nicholas Belton, 74 (top); Andrew Cribb, 44 (bottom), 126 (bottom); Dirkr, 102 (top); Laura Eisenberg, 102 (middle); Elena, 44 (middle); Jill Fromer, 14 (middle); Hlinkazsolt, 126 (top); itographer, 74 (middle); Irina Ivanova, 14 (bottom); Simon Oxley, 74 (bottom); Rusian Pantyushin, 44 (top); Arne Thaysen, 102 (bottom); Ivonne Wierink-vanWetten, 7

Frances Janisch: 139

Ray Kachatorian: 60 (bottom), 109, 157 (bottom left)

Keller & Keller: 21, 22

Michael Luppino: 6, 18, 28, 32, 47, 51, 52, 60 (top), 65, 72 & 73, 76, 78, 89 (top), 111, 113, 132 (left), 133, 136, 140, 152 (bottom right & left), 155 (bottom left)

Charles Maraia: 62, 84 (right), 85, 135 (left), 150

Steven Mays: 91, 155 (top left)

Andrew McCaul: 1, 104, 151 (top left, bottom right), 152 (top right)

Ellen McDermott: 92

Keith Scott Morton: 2, 8, 9, 14 (top), 15, 24, 26 & 27, 29, 30, 31, 34 & 35, 46, 48, 54 & 55, 56 (left), 59, 61, 67, 68, 70, 71, 75, 80, 86, 87, 88, 89 (bottom), 93, 107, 112, 114, 115, 116, 117, 124 & 125, 126 (middle), 127, 129, 130, 135 (right), 137, 151 (top right, bottom left), 153, 155 (top right) , 157 (bottom right)

Laura Moss: 103

Steven Randazzo: 82, 90 (top), 141

Jeremy Samuelson: 58, 63, 138, 143 (bottom), 157 (top left)

William P. Steele: 53, 56 (right), 64, 100 & 101, 134, 154 (bottom), 155 (bottom right), 156 (bottom left)

Robin Stubbert: 11, 12 & 13, 57, 81

William Waldron: 17

Jessie Walker: 131

Wendell T. Webber: 77

Paul Whicheloe: 152 (top left)

Cover: iStock: Ines Koleva (ribbons), Spiderplay (floral fabric)

Front Cover: Lucas Allen (upper and lower right corner); iStock: Ivan Ivanov (key), Subjug (vintage postcard frame); New York Public Library (vintage drawing); Keith Scott Morton (lower left corner)

Spine: iStock: Peter Nguyen (bouquet)

Back Cover: Robbin Stubbert (lower right corner)

index